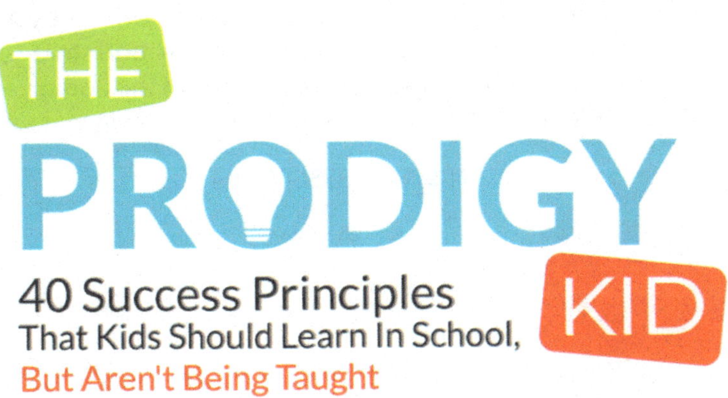

By Jeff Mansen

ISBN-978-1-7335605-0-4

This book is dedicated to ALL the kids who are going to take this wisdom and do great things with their lives!

Table of Contents:

Preface:

The book you are holding can change your life. It can change the lives of the people around you, and it can change the world if used properly. The ingredients for anything that you want out of life lie within the pages of this book.

Most people spend their entire life not knowing the information contained in these pages. They spend their life unaware of the power of how to think, act, and dream big! Some people will use a few of the principles to their benefit, but never understand the tremendous power of using all of them.

When all the principles are used together, they will open the door to anything you desire. In your hands, at a VERY early age, you hold the key to making your dreams come true.

By picking up this book, and learning the golden wisdom contained herein, you can be one of the ones who will have anything you want out of life.

I have spent over 20 years learning the wisdom contained in this book, but you don't have to. With this book, you can start applying these principles immediately, putting you YEARS ahead of where you would have been! Learning and applying this information has changed my life forever; it WILL change yours as well!

Good luck. May all your dreams come true!

Introduction:

One of the tricks to having a happy and fulfilling life that flows as nature intended can be learned from a tree. A tree will start as a seed, turn into a sapling, and then grow larger and larger until one day its life is over.

Observe how nature works, then do the same. Instead of continuing to grow like a tree, most people will go through school and quit growing once they leave. To keep growing, you always need to feed your mind with new things, new challenges, new goals, and new wisdom. Continue to push yourself to grow your whole life, just like a tree. JUST BECAUSE OUR BODIES QUIT GROWING DOESN'T MEAN WE ARE DONE.

The tree has a PURPOSE: To grow into a tree. It starts as a seed and ends up a giant structure that produces thousands of seeds during its lifetime.

It should be your goal to find your purpose, to find your special seed that you are responsible for growing. Realize that your seed can grow just like an acorn grows into a mighty tree.

The key is to never quit learning, and always strive to become the best person you can be. Become the, "tree", that you are meant to be!

To live your life for your purpose will give you more satisfaction than just going through life not knowing what you want out of it. That is the trick with humans; we must discover our seed. We must figure out what our passions are, what we are good at, what we like. Each of us is different.

We can decide if we want to be an oak, a palm or a fruit tree. We can pick our seed, or our starting point, by uncovering what drives our passions the most.

What wonderful thing can you offer the world? What will make you the happiest and give you the most pleasure? What is your purpose, your seed?

There is a REALLY GOOD chance that if you are even reading this book, you have a BIG SEED to offer the world. What could that be?

The information in the following pages will help you figure it out!

Are YOU ready to give YOUR kid an unfair advantage in Life?

Parents go to ProdigyKidBlueprint.com for the next steps.

“If you can dream it, you can do it.”

- Walt Disney

DEALING WITH PEOPLE IN LIFE IS LIKE THROWING A BOOMERANG. WHAT YOU PUT OUT IS WHAT YOU GET BACK.

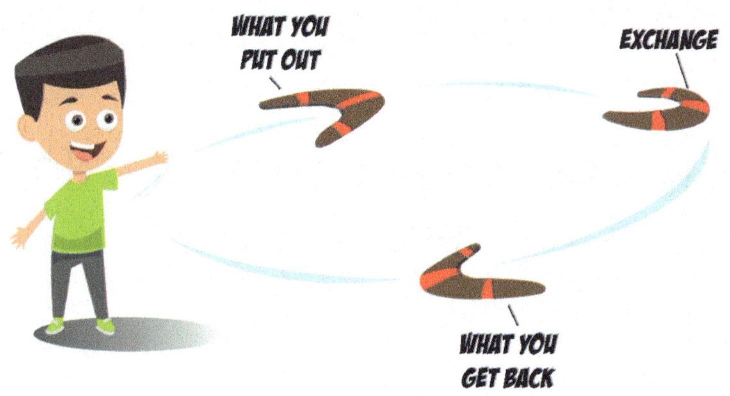

THE GOLDEN RULE

Chapter 1. The Golden Rule

Treat other people the way you want to be treated. Known as the Golden Rule, it is the most important principle. Maybe you have heard it said this way, "What goes around comes around". You can also say that if you are a jerk to people, you can expect that people will be a jerk to you; if you are cool to people, people will be cool to you.

One thing is for certain, the world is filled with PEOPLE! You will always see them, interact with them, and be around them. Try going to the beach, or school, or to the game, or park, or the store, or anywhere where there are no people; it is impossible!

Because you will always be around people, you must accept that to get the most out of life, the most important thing you need to know is how to properly deal with people.

There are many ways to have a good experience with people, but the Golden Rule is key. Here's how it works. How you deal with other people is like a boomerang. When you throw a boomerang, it goes out, then makes a turn and comes right back to you. Guess what? The same can be said of how you treat other people. If you treat other people badly, they will treat you badly. By treating other people well, naturally, they will want to treat you well.

There are times when you may treat people well, but they are still treating you badly. It is not OK, but over your lifetime, it works out in your favor. Those who treat you badly will have more people treat them the same way.

Sometimes, it may be frustrating because all people do not understand or live by the Golden Rule, but it works! Over your lifetime, you will meet those who talk about bad things always happening to them when it comes to people, and you will hear of others who have good things happen to them when it comes to people. It all comes down to how you treat others.

Over the long term, it works like a mirror; you get what you give, and so give others what you would want them to give you.

Over the long term, it works like a mirror; you get what you give, and so give others what you would want them to give you.

Principle 1 – The Golden Rule: To make your goals and dreams come true, you will need all of the help you can get, so always plant the seeds you want to grow. If you plant mean seeds with people, you will grow mean in your life. If you plant nice seeds with people, you will grow nice in your life. You control what you want to grow. What would you rather grow, mean or nice?

Notes

KNOWLEDGE + WISDOM

LEARNING HOW TO THINK + NORMAL LEARNING

MORE KNOWLEDGE + MORE WISDOM

YOU HAVE TO LEARN HOW TO THINK

Chapter 2: You Have to Learn How to Think

How you think is an especially important part of your journey to success. You could set off on a journey to learn anything, and you could do it. But what if I told you that you could learn how to think to TURBO CHARGE your results?

By learning how to think, you can achieve your goals and dreams much faster. The mind is an amazing tool that is just like a muscle. The more you use and strengthen it, the stronger and more effective it will be.

By thinking the way most successful people think, you will become a successful thinker too, and all the possibilities in the world will open up to you.

A prodigy is someone who naturally thinks differently than the average person. For example, prodigies are usually under 10, but perform at abilities way beyond their age and experience compared to an average person. It would be great if they would let us know how they did it, but they were already like that.

Unless we are born a prodigy, it's hard to suddenly turn into one, but there is hope.

There are countless stories of people who came from very humble beginnings and rose to extreme success with their lives and careers. They did not start out as prodigies but ended up more successful than most people. What we can do is learn how they think. There are thousands of books written about the successes that people have had, as well as autobiographies of these successful people. Guess what? By studying them and reading their books, we can figure out how they think, how they may have started out homeless and rose to great success. What did they think? What habits did they have? How did they act? Once we figure out their secrets, we can apply them to our situation. That's what this book is all about, giving you 40 of the most important ways to think based on research of what has made others super successful!

Think about it like this: Your brain is like a computer and how you think is like your software. By learning and using the principles within this book, you will be installing successful thinking software into your mind (Your computer). Computers are always updating their software with the latest version. You must continue to align your thinking with proper success thought patterns.

Professional athletes can be a great example of how to think. They have learned and practiced hard at their particular sports. They also have coaches who help them practice every day to fine-tune their skills and abilities. They have worked hard, but they also think differently than an average athlete or amateur player. The way they think is key to their success.

The discipline of how they think is what allows them to achieve monumental success. What are they thinking right before a big play, and right after? That would be great information to have if you want to strive to push your athletic ability to its limits.

Your excitement to achieve your goals and dreams should also be transferred to your desire to learn how to make them come true. As you learn what it takes, you should feel joy in the fact that you are slowly making it happen!

Principle 2: You Have to Learn How to Think. Learning how to think is simple, but not all thinking is the same, and not all ways of thinking are the same. By learning this and the other principles in this book, you will learn and be able to use some of the most effective and important ways of thinking that have guided people who have had success in reaching their goals and dreams.

Notes

I WANT TO, BUT DON'T THINK I CAN.

I THINK I CAN, BUT DON'T WANT TO.

I WANT TO AND I BELIEVE I CAN!

BURNING DESIRE AND BELIEF

Chapter 3 Burning Desire and Belief

It's not enough to believe you can accomplish your goals; you must also want to accomplish them. The more you want your goals to happen, the greater chance they WILL happen.

You can have goals and dreams, but if you don't really want them, they won't come true. Or you can want them to come true, but you don't believe you can make it happen. That little act of doubt or lack of desire will hurt your chances of achieving success.

You must create a BURNING DESIRE to want your dreams to come true. Making your dreams come true is no easy road. It is hard work, so you must feel what you really want in your heart. There must be NO doubt in what you want to accomplish.

The world is full of untapped potential, and the possibilities are endless. It is up to you to connect the dots. You must find the pieces and put them together like a puzzle. Even if it seems impossible, you must believe you can do it, because the connections you need are there!

Your belief that you can accomplish your goals and dreams should be so strong that you can almost, "feel", what it would feel like if your accomplished them. Your thinking should be that the only way you won't accomplish them is if you quit, otherwise it will become a reality.

How much BURNING DESIRE do you need? This BURNING DESIRE you need to make your dreams come true can be defined by this awesome story I heard once.

This kid just out of college, met this rich tycoon and wanted to be a rich tycoon too. The kid asked the tycoon if he could teach him how to be a rich tycoon.

The rich tycoon felt like helping this kid, so he agreed. He said, "You have to not only believe you can do it, you have to have a burning desire to make it happen."

The rich tycoon invited the kid to get started the next day. He told the kid to meet him at the beach the next morning at 5a.m.

The next day, the kid shows up at precisely at 5a.m. dressed in a suit, tie and nice shoes. The rich tycoon is wearing a tee shirt, flip flops, and swimming trunks. The kid is a little confused and says, "I thought you were going to teach me how to be a rich tycoon?"

The rich tycoon said, "Let's start." He walked up to his knees in the water, and said, "Follow me." The kid, wanting to learn, took off his shoes and walked into the water up to his knees wearing his nice business clothes.

The rich tycoon walked further into the water to his chest and asked the kid to follow him. There they were at 5a.m. in the morning, chest deep in the water, and suddenly the rich tycoon grabbed the kid and pushed his head under the water. The kid was thrashing around trying to get above water to breathe. After about 10 seconds of this, the rich tycoon let him up and, gasping for air the kid yelled, "WHY DID YOU DO THAT?" The rich tycoon said, "When you were under the water thinking you were going to drown, what did you want?" The kid said, "AIR!" The tycoon said, "How bad did you want the air?" The kid said, "REALLY BAD!"

The rich tycoon said, "If you want your goals and dreams to come true, it takes a lot of work and dedication. You must believe you can accomplish them. You must have a BURNING DESIRE to make them come true just like you wanted air when you were under the water."

There must be no doubts of your intentions!

Principle 3: Burning Desire and Belief. The key to achieving your goals and dreams is that you must create a BURNING DESIRE to get them, and, just as important, you must BELIEVE you can make your dreams come true. BURNING DESIRE and BELIEF are two, important building blocks you need to make your goals and dreams come true.

Notes

TODAY
CALENDAR:
NOW
TODAY: HOW
THINGS ARE NOW
WATCH IT EVERYDAY +
MAKE IT BETTER
MOVIE OF
PERFECT LIFE
CALENDAR:
FUTURE WHEN
GOALS & DREAMS
COME TRUE
WHEN YOUR
DREAMS ARE TRUE
FEEL THE HAPPINESS AND
GRADITUDE IN YOUR HEART
AS IF IT HAS ALREADY HAPPENED
THE MOVIE IN YOUR MIND

Chapter 4 The Movie in Your Mind

Imagine how you want your perfect life to be when you grow up, creating a "movie in your mind." Every time you think about your perfect life, you are, "reviewing", the movie that you created. Every time you imagine it, you edit some of the scenes so that it becomes clearer.

Your mind is capable of more powerful things than you may realize. You have one of the world's most powerful computers between your ears. When it comes to making your dreams come true, your imagination is key.

Some kids like riding horses, some like to skateboard, some like going to the beach, some like hanging out with friends, some like hiking in the mountains. We all have different things we like. Even siblings can like different things. You must find what you like and want out of life.

If everything were perfect, how would it be? Sometimes, we are born into situations that are not perfect. Although it can be frustrating as a kid, the older you get, the more you can control exactly how you want everything to be. That means that if you are living in a less than perfect life, IT IS ONLY TEMPORARY IF YOU WANT IT TO BE! It is kind of a trick as a kid, because sometimes it seems like you are stuck where you are, but you hold the key to your perfect life! Creating a movie in your mind is an important step to imagining your life after you have reached your goals. Don't focus on the bad stuff, focus on the good stuff to come.

Imagine what your perfect day looks like. Where do you wake up? What does your room look like? What is for breakfast? What do you do? Where do you go? Who are you with? You cannot go backwards. Let's say you no longer have your dog that you love; that is so sad to me. But what you have to do instead of imagining your old dog in your perfect day, is imagine a new one that you will also love just as much.

As you imagine your perfect day, you are creating a movie in your mind. The more times you watch a movie, the more you know what will happen next. The more times you imagine your perfect day, it becomes clearer and clearer. You know what happens next.

Just like imagining your perfect day, you can imagine your perfect life. What are you going to be when you grow up? What kind of house will you have? What kind of stuff will you do? It is up to you! As a kid, you have almost UNLIMITED CHOICES of how your life can be. Why not choose exactly what YOU want out of life?

It may be hard at first, but this is how to come up with dreams. You can't make your dreams come true if you don't have a clear vision of them, almost like a movie in your mind.

Every time you play this movie in your mind, you create a deeper layer of focus, and the more the universe will work with you to put it together. When you, "play this movie", imagine the feeling of joy and happiness of how you would feel if it was real, because in your mind it is real!

Once you get the hang of creating the movie in your mind, you are ready for the next part of the movie-in-your-mind making process. You HAVE to imagine it like it already happened. It may seem strange, but that is how it works! You have to, "feel it in your heart", that it is real. You have to have joy and be grateful that your goals and dreams are already a reality. YOUR DREAMS HAVE TO HAPPEN IN YOUR MIND BEFORE THEY CAN HAPPEN IN REAL LIFE.

Instead of thinking, "I want to be a doctor", the movie in your mind is, "I am a doctor". Imagine all of the people you are helping, and how that makes you feel.

The movie in your mind is meant to stretch your imagination.

Principle 4: The Movie in Your Mind. Review the movie in your mind daily. When you play the movie in your mind over and over, you will start to feel it in your heart. That is when you will know that it is going to become real because in your mind it already has.

HOW NATURE WORKS
GROWING A CARROT
PLANT A SEED
IN TIME WITH NUTURING TURNS INTO WHAT YOU WANT.
WHAT YOUR INTENTION IS WHEN PLANTING A SEED.
"GROWING" YOUR GOALS AND DREAMS
GOALS AND DREAMS
IN TIME WITH NUTURING TURNS INTO WHAT YOU WANT.
GOALS AND DREAMS ACCOMPLISHED!
WRITING YOU GOALS DOWN IS LIKE PLANTING A SEED.
YOU HAVE TO KNOW WHAT YOUR END RESULT WILL BE, AND YOU HAVE TO WRITE IT DOWN.
BEGIN WITH THE END IN MIND

Chapter 5 Begin with the End in Mind

When you plant a carrot seed, you know the result will be the carrot. How will you know if you are heading in the right direction if you don't know where you are going?

The theory of making your dreams come true is that you first need to know what your dreams are. Just like planting a carrot seed, the end goal is to grow a carrot.

Believe it or not, most people go through life not really knowing what they want. They spend more time planning where they are going on vacations than planning where they are going in life. You ABSOLUTELY need to know where you are going so that you use the right map.

Can you imagine going on vacation, driving for hours in a random direction, then spending vacation where you end up? You can't even go to the airport and fly anywhere unless you buy a ticket to somewhere!

YOU MUST CHOOSE A DESTINATION FOR YOUR LIFE!

Once you have figured out what it is that you want, whether it's a small goal, or the goals for your whole life, you can work backwards from the end result to figure out what you need to do to make them happen.

For example, if you are interested in helping people and would like to become a doctor, you can ask a doctor how to do it. They won't give you a map but will probably tell you something like, "study and get good grades, go to medical school and graduate, do an internship and open a practice". Those are very broad directions that have to be made into more details.

There is a lot that goes into each step. The ways you need to study, what you should study, major tests to take, extra things that students do to help get into college like volunteering, figuring out what type of doctor you want to be, are all part the end goal on top of getting good grades.

You must keep breaking down the plan until you have small goals that are easy to achieve. Small goals like studying about the human body for an hour every day after school or waking up an hour earlier to study.

By having a map, or a plan for your life, you know if you are on track and what the next steps are. Let's say you want to be in the medical field. That means you will take the advanced anatomy class instead of underwater basket weaving class in school. While making baskets might be easier than learning about the body, it's not a part of your map.

Principle 5: Begin with the End in Mind. Just like the carrot and anything else you want to grow in your life, your ideas dreams and goals are like seeds. You have to know what seeds you want to plant in your life in order to grow your goals and dreams.

Notes

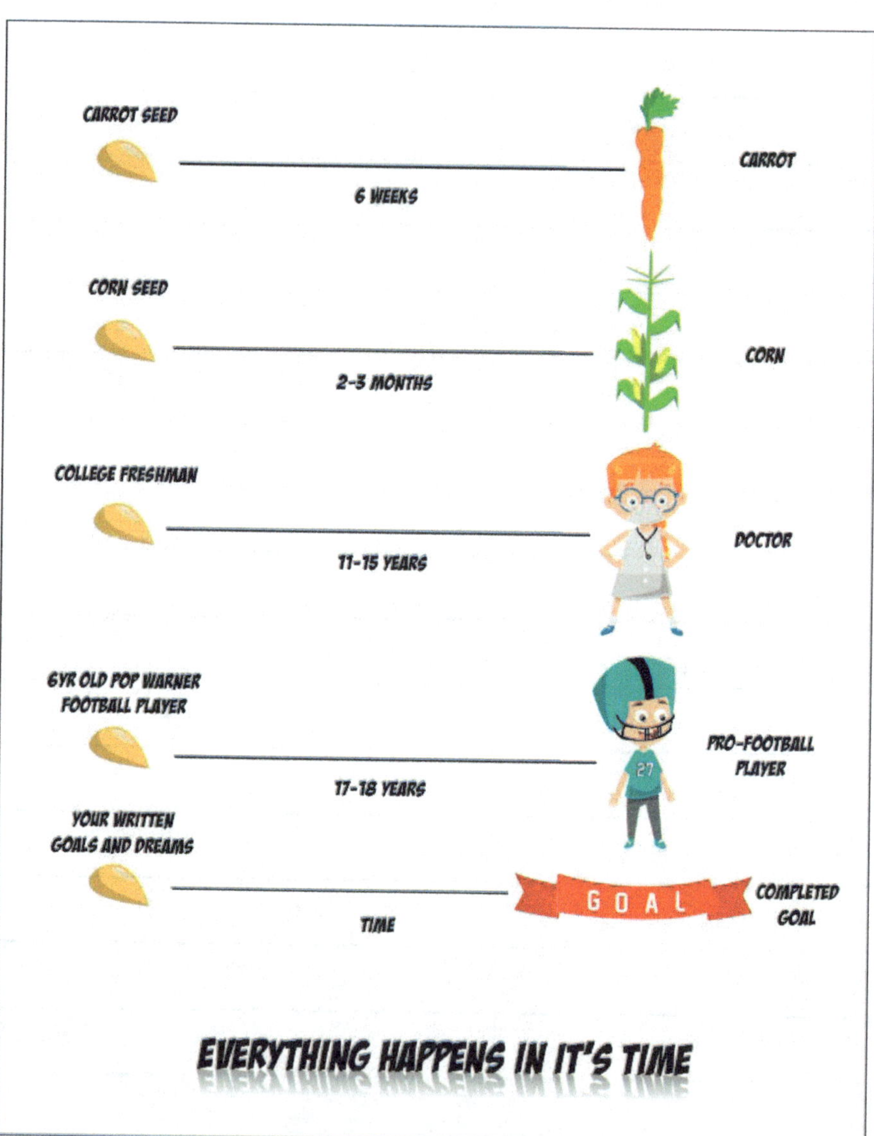
CARROT SEED
6 WEEKS
CARROT
CORN SEED
2-3 MONTHS
CORN
COLLEGE FRESHMAN
11-15 YEARS
DOCTOR
6YR OLD POP WARNER
FOOTBALL PLAYER
17-18 YEARS
27
PRO-FOOTBALL
PLAYER
YOUR WRITTEN
GOALS AND DREAMS
TIME
GOAL
COMPLETED
GOAL
EVERYTHING HAPPENS IN IT'S TIME

Chapter 6 Everything Happens in It's Time

All goals and dreams have a time attached to them. Naturally, smaller goals have less time, and larger goals have more time that it takes to accomplish them.

This principle can be compared to the difference between cooking a chicken wing in the oven and cooking the whole chicken. The whole chicken will always take longer than cooking a wing, even though, technically, it's chicken. When it comes to how long something will take, many things can affect the timing of it. The thing that always remains is, there is always an end time.

Growing food is the best way to see the law of how everything happens in it's time in nature. Seeds must be properly planted to start the timing of growth, and the seeds must be properly nurtured throughout their growing duration.

For example:

Radishes are ready to pick in about 30 days

Pole beans take about 60-70 days

Corn takes about 60-90 days

Some varieties of oranges take up to a year from bloom to being ripe!

In 30 days, when your radishes begin to ripen, your ripe oranges will still be a long way off.

Here's where it gets tricky: The same types of foods can take different times to grow even though they are the SAME plant! In the same sense, people may have similar or the same goals, but they may take different times to achieve for each person.

It depends on you! You are in control of your situation. Just because someone says something can't be done, or it will take a certain time, doesn't mean it HAS to take that long. Maybe for them, it would be impossible or take forever, but you might be able to do it at a quicker pace.

An important concept to realize is that sometimes, people may choose a goal or dream that isn't their seed, but they think it is. If you want to be a professional basketball player, and you are short, you have to realize that you can still be very good and have lots of fun, but professional basketball players are mostly tall. So, being a professional basketball player may not be YOUR seed.

Here is another example about timing. Walking to school takes more time than riding a bike, which takes more time than driving. The method you choose depends on the methods available to you and how fast you want to get to school. Once you know what your goals and dreams are, you then figure out your how, then you can put timing to it. As you see, from the above with methods for getting to school, there are also different methods for achieving your goals and dreams. Some things are constant while others can be affected by how you approach them.

You just need to understand that there is a basic law that causes your goals and dreams to grow to fruition. Growing a garden is the simplest way to show how this works. It is up to you to figure out the best way to do it and figure out your timing of achieving them.

Principle 6: Everything Happens in Its Time. Even though there are many variables in achieving your goals, you must set a target date to achieve the goal or dream. You have to work to achieve it by that date. If it doesn't happen by the set date, then you must evaluate why the target date was missed. Don't give up; instead, adjust your target date and work hard to achieve it. There is no failure unless you stop trying.

Notes

GARDENING

EQUAL TO

GROWING YOUR GOALS AND DREAMS

WRITE GOALS DOWN (PLANT SEED)

NURTURE: READ ALOUD DAILY, REVIEW, REVISE, TAKE ACTION

END GOAL + DREAM ACHIEVED

WRITE YOUR GOALS DOWN

Chapter 7 Write Your Goals Down

Why should you write down goals? Because what was once an idea in your mind, when written, can be physically seen. That little act of writing it down is your first ACTION toward making your goals happen.

Once you have a good idea of your dreams and goals, the next step is to write them down.

Successful people write down their goals. The best thing to do is to get a journal or plain notebook. I call it your magic notebook.

Your magic notebook is where your dream takes shape. Any thought that you have exists in another dimension until it is put on paper. The key is putting what is in your head on paper. If you keep your plans and ideas in your head, you may soon forget that idea and never act.

When you write down your goals, plans, and ideas in a notebook, it gets the ball rolling. What do you do next? You commit to create a daily habit of writing down your goals, plans, and ideas. This daily habit becomes part of your life, and slowly your vision for your future will become clearer.

Use the power of your mind for your benefit. By writing down your goals, plans, and ideas regularly, you actually can trick your subconscious mind into believing whatever it is that you tell it. In case you are unsure of what your subconscious mind is, it is the part of your mind that runs your whole body without you having to think about it. It tells your heart to beat, breathes for you, and handles all kinds of processes you need not worry about. It is your, "auto-pilot".

By writing your goals and dreams down regularly, you are slowly programming your auto-pilot to help steer you to achieve your goals and dreams.

Another tip is to write your goals, plans, and dreams as if they've already happened and you are living them. Instead of "I want to be successful," write "I am successful." "I want to be on the team" becomes "I am on the team."

Of course, there are things that may or may not happen, no matter how many times you write them down, but by writing your goals, plans, and ideas down, you increase your chances of success. Nothing is guaranteed!

Keep this in mind also – you must be realistic. No matter how many times you write it down, you won't be able to fly, lift a 1,000 pound boulder with your index finger, have x-ray vision, or have ESP. But you can lose weight, or eat better, make more money, or become a better student. The Universe wants you to achieve your life's mission more than you do.

Through the practice of regularly writing in your magic notebook, you begin to think really big about life and going after your dreams. By writing new material into your magic notebook, faithfully reviewing it and TAKING ACTION, your future goals and plans become a part of you. As you build on your goals and plans by reviewing them every day, they become your special seed.

I have been following this principle for years, and I am amazed when I go back to review old notebooks. I realize that I've accomplished things that were once only ideas that I had written down, and are now real goals that have been achieved!

Principle 7: Write Your Goals Down. Write down your goals, add to them and review them daily. You have the ability to achieve anything humanly possible that you write down as long as you are willing to put do the work. By following the principles I have laid out, you have the tools to achieve your goals and dreams.

Notes

THIS PERSON WOULD BE HAPPY WITH $100,000 PER YEAR

1/10 TO GOAL

$100,000 PER YEAR

THIS PERSON WOULD BE HAPPY WITH $100,000 PER YEAR

1/10 TO GOAL

$10,000 PER YEAR

YOU HAVE TO THINK BIG

Chapter 8 You Have to Think BIG

There is an unexplained secret power behind thinking BIG. Each one of us carries a seed for our own PERFECT life and thinking big is one of the ways to encourage that seed. It is up to us to figure out what type of seed is within us, so we can encourage it to grow to be the best we can be.

What is the biggest, GREATEST thing you can do with your life? Your largest goals should always have good intentions. It should be as if you had a Magic Genie with unlimited wishes.

As you go about the process of figuring out your dreams, there is a magic ingredient you must know about. It is THINKING REALLY BIG.

Thinking BIG will help you to stay focused and motivated.

The life force that grows a carrot will also grow your goals and dreams. By going big, the life force behind it is stronger, increasing the chance of a successful future. Why does a carrot seed grow into a big juicy carrot that you want to eat? You can say it's the water, or sunlight, or soil, but it's the seed, and the life force that makes it grow; the bigger, the better.

If you could predict early in your life that anything you wanted would come true, what would you choose? Would you choose to have only a little money for food and things you like, or unlimited money for anything you wanted? Would you like the world as it is, or would you want to make it better?

This principle is about seeing things for how they can be if everything was perfect, not just how they are now. To imagine your wildest dreams and what your life would be like if they worked out.

Creating a vision for your future is a start! If the idea and vision are there, what else can be there?

By going big, even if you cannot make it all happen, you still did very well. Not everyone is meant to change the world, but everyone can change their world.

If your dream is to earn a lot of money and travel, what comes next once you have achieved those dreams? It's nice to have fancy cars, big houses, the latest toys, lots of vacations, etc., but once you have everything money can buy, will you really feel happy inside? Experience shows that real happiness and peace will come from knowing you are doing all you can to make the world a better place.

Discover what you really like, then strive to be the absolute best at it. Each of these principles is a building block to make that discovery.

Now, you are setting big goals and have created a big vision for your future. That is good, but the way to achieve the big vision is to create small goals that add up to bigger goals that eventually lead to your dreams coming true. Remember the principle "Begin with the End in Mind?" Achieving your dreams takes a big vision with goals to get you to the end.

As my mother used to say when I was young, "If you want something bad enough, the universe will put it together for you." I believed her, but I also have come to realize that by thinking really big, it's easier for the universe to hear what you want.

Principle 8: You Have to Think BIG! Think big to achieve great things. Go big because even though you might not get to the end of your massive dream, at least you didn't sell yourself short. Selling yourself short is much worse than not reaching a massive goal.

Notes

WE ARE "**MAGICALLY**" GUIDED TO OUR GOALS AND DREAMS
IN A SIMILAR WAY, IF WE...
CREATE A WRITTEN STATEMENT AND READ OUT LOUD IN THE MORNING AND AT NIGHT

THE POWER OF AFFIRMATIONS

Chapter 9 The Power of Affirmations

By reading your plans every morning when you wake up, and just before bed, you enable a magnetism of the universe to attract that on which you are focused. Strengthen the magnetism by daily writing your plans and reading them aloud. That's an affirmation.

Your mind only knows what you tell it. The way affirmations work is you write out what your goals and dreams are as if they already happened and you are living them, like the story of how you achieved them.

Pretend you are being interviewed for a T.V. show and are telling the interviewer how you were able to achieve your goals. You would tell the story as if it has already happened.

Each morning upon waking up, and right before bed, read your plan out loud. By doing this, you are suggesting to your mind that your future has already happened. The mind only knows what you tell it. The more times you do it, the more your mind begins to believe it's true.

As you follow this practice, you should have great emotion of joy, love, gratitude, and happiness of knowing your future has come true. It will be true in your mind. You will feel positive emotions with your vision and feel those emotions in your heart.

The more times you do this, the more your plan will strengthen. Imagine the strength of one piece of dental floss. It can break easily. How strong would a thousand pieces of floss, woven together, be? By repeatedly following this practice, your vision becomes stronger and stronger.

As you read it aloud, imagine the feeling of living your dreams and goals, feelings of gratitude, love, joy, happiness. Not only do you need to feel the words as you read them, you need to feel, see, and hear them in your heart as if they are true.

As you grow in the practice of affirmations, it's as if you reach a state of being on auto-pilot when thinking of achieving your goals and dreams. Achieving this state draws you to your desired outcome by helping you to do what you need to do.

Napoleon Hill also understood the power of the mind. In his book, "Think and Grow Rich", he talks about autosuggestion, which is another way to say affirmation. Using affirmations is like a mind trick. You can actually trick your mind into believing that you have already accomplished your goals and dreams. This puts you on a direct course to make it happen.

Napoleon Hill's theory of autosuggestion and affirmation tests the boundaries of what is possible by using the habit of reading your goals and dreams out loud to trick your mind into thinking you have already achieved them.

Napoleon Hill used the example of a homing pigeon to explain how this works. You can drive the bird in a car a thousand miles from home in a covered cage. If you take it out of the cage and throw it up in the air, it will circle a few times, then start flying to its home destination. It is somehow guided to its end goal, which is home.

By repeating your affirmations daily, your mind and the universe will work together to automatically create the byproduct of your goals and dreams. Like the homing pigeon, you will be guided to the destination of your goals and dreams.

Principle 9: The Power of Affirmations. Even though the idea of affirmation may seem silly, why don't you try it before saying it won't work? Write down your goals and dreams. Read them out loud twice daily (Or more) as if they have already happened. See the words, hear your voice reading them, feel the vibration of the words in your throat, and feel them in your heart. It is your life's grandest plan at that moment. You make what was once written on a piece of paper a reality in your life. You speak it into existence.

WHAT?
WHEN?
HOW?
+ BIG
+ PAST STATEMENT + DAILY REVIEW & DAILY REVISIONS
+ ACTION = SUCCESS!
THE MAGIC FORMULA

Chapter 10. The Magic Formula

The basics to achieve goals and dreams can be simplified into a formula. Experience has shown that this formula works to help achieve success. The other steps in The Prodigy Kid will keep you focused, motivated and headed in the direction of your goals. But, these are the basics to understand and master in your journey.

Your goals and dreams are like farming. In farming, there are time-honored rules that farmers have passed down for generations, in addition to science, to successfully grow food. Generations of successful people have also developed rules or principles, to achieve their goals and dreams.

The Magic Formula:

1. Write down your goal. Seeds do not start to grow until they are planted. By writing down your goals and dreams, you are planting their seeds. The seeds will not start to grow until they are planted, as your goals and dreams will not grow until the absolute first step is taken by writing them down.

2. Set a deadline. State EXACTLY when you will complete your goal. There is a time attached to every goal and dream. Just as it will take 2-3 months to grow corn, your goals and dreams will take time to achieve. Use the plan you developed to set a specific date by which to achieve your goal.

3. Organize your goals into a plan, then begin to follow your plan. You cannot have something for nothing; everything worthwhile takes effort and work. A seed needs to be watered. It needs to be planted where it will get sunlight. It may need fertilizer. Work is involved.

4. Think BIG. This is one of the magic ingredients that make the formula work. It is all about discovering what your ultimate goals and dreams are, in a way that they are attainable. For example, you probably won't to be able to travel instantly to other planets, but you could become an astronaut. Another example is growing a garden in your backyard vs. ending world hunger. Ending world hunger would be the big way of thinking compared to a garden in your backyard.

5. Create a written statement of your goals in past tense like it's already happened. Read it out loud when you wake up in the morning, and before going to sleep, and as many times as you can in between. This practice helps to focus on the goal. In a perfect world, when you read it, you are imagining it as if it has already happened. When people tend to their garden daily, sometimes, they can almost taste the food they are growing; they can imagine the snap and crunch of ripe corn as they eat it. Write your goal as if you have achieved it. This is called affirmation.

6. Review and revise your plan daily as you figure out what works; educate yourself on what you need to know and do to make your plan work. You can plant a seed in your garden, but what happens if you don't check on it? Your garden will get better each year as you figure out little things that make it grow better. Some plants do better where it's very dry, while others prefer damp conditions. The tomatoes may grow better with a post to help hold them up. There will always be more experienced and knowledgeable gardeners whom you can ask questions. There are farming almanacs, books and magazines, and online where you can learn better techniques. This is an example of how to educate yourself about the direction your goal will take you.

7. If you have constructed your plan correctly, you will have daily steps to work on and results to track. Just like gardening, if you

don't tend your plan, it could die of neglect. Distractions can destroy it. Your plan needs small action steps that are completed daily and build on achieving the ultimate goal of success.

Principle 10: The Magic Formula. What + When + How + Big + Statement + Review/ Revise + ACTION = SUCCESS!

YOU ATTRACT WHAT YOU THINK ABOUT AND FOCUS ON
THINK BAD STUFF
WHAT YOU THINK
BAD
ATTRACTS
STUFF
THINK GOOD STUFF
WHAT YOU THINK
GOOD
ATTRACTS
STUFF
THE LAW OF ATTRACTION

Chapter 11 The Law of Attraction

Simply put, the Law of Attraction is the ability to attract whatever we are focusing on into our lives.

The Law of Attraction is the belief that you bring what you focus on into your life. If you focus on good stuff, you bring good stuff into your life. If you focus on bad stuff, you bring bad stuff into your life. It is called a law, but in fact, it is a time-tested theory that many notable people have used to explain the positive experiences in their lives.

The Law says that with the help of a very powerful Universe, what you can think in your mind can be transformed into a physical reality.

Like a magnet, if you are always thinking about your goals and dreams, the theory says you will attract them.

Like a magnet, if you are always thinking about the worst things happening, the theory says that your goals and dreams won't come true, and you will attract doom and gloom.

The key is to focus on what you want, and not focus on anything harmful, destructive, negative, or mean.

There are some people who say it isn't a law since it is merely a theory, but it has been taught and used for thousands of years. Over the past 100 years, it has been taught more extensively, with many people using it to make their goals and dreams come true.

Traditional teachings believe that nothing in life comes free, but only from hard work; however, another school of thought will argue that the mere act of thinking in a way that lines up your goals and dreams is action towards making them come true because of the Law of Attraction.

The following is a complex example to illustrate the Law of Attraction. It may be complex, but I have broken it down so you can understand it.

The new quantum physics is beginning to shed light on this concept with the fact that we are part of a complex energy system that is pure potential. Some areas of investigation are discovering that everything is energy, including our thoughts. Our thoughts can connect with the energy of the universe, giving us access to pure potential. Think about your brain working the way a smart phone works. You can turn on your phone and receive a video through thin air directly to your phone as a signal from the cell towers. You can't see it happening, the same way that your brain connects with the energy of the universe to influence the outcome of your thoughts.

Man-made computers and cell phones haven't been around very long compared to the vastness and complexity of the Universe. The idea that your thoughts are working with the universe to determine how your life will turn out has been around for thousands of years.

Principle 11: The Law of Attraction. The Law of Attraction is a powerful force. If you accept that this concept could be true, then you should practice it by thinking positive thoughts for yourself and for the world around you. Through this practice, you can attract your goals and dreams into your life!

Notes

BY DAILY REVIEWING, REVISING, AND REPEATING THE PROCESS YOUR VISION BECOMES CLEARER, AND YOU GET CLOSER TO YOUR GOALS AND DREAMS.

REVIEW, REVISE, AND TALK ABOUT YOUR GOALS AND DREAMS.

Chapter 12. Review, Revise, and Talk About Your Goals and Dreams

Have you gotten your Magic Notebook and started writing down your goals and dreams in life? Writing them down is the first step in perfecting them. As you review and adjust what you wrote the day before and take the time to rewrite them, the repetitive action reinforces your thoughts and strengthens your goals in your conscience and subconscious mind (auto pilot).

By rewriting and refining your goals, two things will happen: You will naturally be making your plans better, and your plans will become clearer to you. As they become clearer, you will feel an excitement and enthusiasm that will have you talking about them to other people.

When your plan is so clear that you are telling other people about it, that action will create even more excitement.

Having big goals and dreams is awesome, but as time passes and your situation changes, your goals and dreams should be fluid, so they can change too. It's OK to revise what you have written in your magic notebook. When you change interests in life, or as you get older, change your goals and dreams to match your new interests.

When you start talking about your goals with others, be prepared for criticism and negative responses. It takes time and effort to uncover the true seed of your goals and dreams. If people are negative, it is very important remain positive. Don't take other people's criticism personally, look for the wisdom.

Another challenge you may face is reaching dead ends when trying to plan your goals and dreams. That is why daily revisions are so cool! As you learn and figure new things out, it's a sign of growth to abandon ideas that are not as good, for those that are much better. Maybe others are correct in their doubts and criticism. Sometimes they are, but sometimes they are not! Don't let people who may be jealous or not want you to succeed cause you to change your mind; keep pushing forward and forget those who do not support you.

Things change. In football, sometimes a quarterback's goal is to throw the ball way down the field to make the next play, but at the last minute, he has to run instead. Your plans may not always be perfect, but always be ready to take steps forward, even if they aren't the big steps you would have liked.

Principle 12: Review, Revise, Talk About Your Goals and Dreams. When you review, revise, and talk about your goals and dreams, you are working and stretching your creative muscles. As you do this consistently over a lifetime, you will open the doors to your pure potential, where anything is possible for you and your life. It is within this pure potential that anything is possible!

Notes

DREAMS
&
GOALS

DREAMS
&
GOALS

Chapter 13 ACTION!

YOU NEED TO GET BUSY! You can have the GREATEST IDEA IN THE WORLD, but without action, it is just an idea. Any step in the right direction is action. The more steps in the right direction, the faster the idea will come true.

Action is the fuel that makes everything work. In previous steps such as the movie in your mind, you have learned that writing, daily reviewing, revising, and reading out loud your written goals and dreams are key to creating a vision and a plan. However, action is the only thing that makes it all possible.

Your idea might be to create something awesome and better than anything anyone has ever seen, but if you don't do anything with the idea, it isn't real.

Getting started on the right actions to take may require you to do research. Find someone who has done something similar to what you want to do and ask them how they did it. Use their steps to start working toward your own idea or dream. There is so much information online, with some research, you will be able to figure out some—if not all—of the steps you will need.

Sometimes, you may be doing something new that nobody has ever done. That is where creating your steps may be tricky. You may have too many steps, they may be out of order, and some may be the wrong ones. The important lesson to remember is that you must apply ACTION and you will begin to see what the most logical next step is. Even if you take a step or two backwards, doing so can help you to take new steps forward!

Once you begin to move forward to your dreams, a key principle is to not stop. It is very easy to do really good for a short period of time, then slack off. DON'T DO THIS! Make a commitment to doing something that is on your action list every day. Don't let yourself off the hook.

For example, I wrote this book you are reading in the early morning before the sun came up. In order for my goals and dreams to become a reality, I had to write this book. One of my steps was to wake up daily at 5:30 a.m. and write 500-1000 words for the book. A second daily step was to work on building my websites. Before most people even begin their days, I had been writing and working on websites for a couple of hours.

I was getting things done every day. I couldn't look back to the starting line and see success, I was experiencing and feeling success each day as I consistently moved my project forward one step at a time towards the finish line.

There were earlier times when I would be committed for a week straight, or a couple of days, then I would put my writing down for a while. This was better than nothing, but it wasn't enough to keep the magic happening every day.

I had my overall plan, and my step was to work on it daily, but I found myself stuck between envisioning the goals and dreams to actually applying ACTION to them. I had to make a revision to my steps to include waking up at 5:30, and immediately going to the computer and start writing EVERY DAY, no matter how sick or tired I felt.

As I was writing, about a quarter of the way through, I added a step to review what I wrote earlier in the day and revise it. That way, when I was done, I didn't have to go back to revise and edit all of it at one time.

It took a lot for me to go from writing my goals and dreams down to applying action daily in a consistent way. I had to make changes to how I approached achieving my goals by taking steps every day.

John Maxwell has written about the concept of failing forward. That means it is OK to make mistakes as you learn. You will NEVER move forward if you do not try things you have never done before. When you have not done it before, you could fail in your first attempt. The important lesson is to pick yourself up, learn why you fell, and move forward again with new confidence.

Principle 13: ACTION! Daily Action is the key to making your dreams and goals come true. As my personal example shows, reaching your goals and dreams takes WORK! Putting in the time and effort by applying ACTION to your plan is the way forward; otherwise, it is only a plan on a piece of paper.

TRUTH + HONESTY IS LIKE WATER.
JUST LIKE WATER WILL FIND THE LOWEST POINT,
THE TRUTH WILL ALWAYS BE FOUND.

HONESTY

Chapter 14 Honesty

None of the principles in this book will work for you without honesty. Fewer opportunities will come your way if people cannot trust you, so you decrease your chances for true wealth and success in life than if you were just truthful and ALWAYS do the right thing!

Honesty is an important part of being successful. To realize your goals and dreams, you must be honest. That means always doing the right thing, even when no one is looking, because in the end, you will always know.

You cannot lie to yourself. Knowing you were dishonest will turn off the pure potential that you could have had.

Being honest is like water. Water will always find the lowest point, and the truth will always be found out. If the truth always comes out, the only thing being dishonest will get you is a little more time before you are found out.

Another way honesty is like water is when it runs through a garden hose. Water will flow out, but if you fold it in half, it will stop or barely trickle out. The same goes for your goals and dreams; if you are dishonest, your opportunities will barely trickle or stop completely.

It is ALWAYS better to be honest upfront, even if there are severe consequences. Severe consequences are worse if dishonesty is involved.

If you lie, cheat, and steal, you can forget about principles in The Prodigy Kid working for you. You may have some form of success over the years, but it can and will usually be taken from you. Everything can be perfect, but dishonesty will ruin everything you have worked for in a second.

You can work hard for many years and lose all of your progress INSTANTLY with dishonesty.

You can lie to people, but you still know the truth. You can cheat, and you still know you don't deserve to win. You can steal from people, but you still know it is not yours.

Principle 14: Honesty When it comes to making your dreams and goals come true, be honest with others and be honest with yourself.

Notes

ALL THE POSSIBILITIES IN THE WORLD

THE BIGGER YOUR BOOKSHELVES, THE BIGGER YOUR POTENTIAL

YOU HAVE TO BE AN AVID LEARNER

Chapter 15 You Have to Be an Avid Learner

One of the best habits you can develop is to become an avid learner and gain a love for learning. One thing that the most successful people have in common is a large collection of books that they have read. There is something magical about reading and learning that gives you the confidence to pursue anything you choose, even if you don't know how. You can ALWAYS learn it.

The best way to put a halt to succeeding in your life is to quit learning. It might be hard to quit learning though; life is a journey that allows you to experience and learn new things daily. The journey to your goals and dreams requires that you learn and potentially practice what you learn for YEARS!

You cannot expect to know how to do something without first learning how. Something as easy as eating must be learned. I was amazed when I realized that people that living in China do not use forks and spoons. But I was not raised to eat with chopsticks, and I do not and cannot use them. Can you imagine all of the other things that are learned that we don't even think about?

You can do anything that you decide to do if you want to do it. But the trick is you have to learn how to do it first. The good news is that you can research and find out information about how to do almost everything that anyone has ever done.

The internet has given us access to so much more than books. We have, at a click of a button, knowledge in the form of videos, podcasts, blogs, online courses, and books. The internet has created networking opportunities and groups that you can join, with a wealth of knowledge not available to generations before the internet.

Successful people have one thing in common—they love to learn and are big readers. Business coach and motivational speaker Brian Tracy recommends reading 500 books on any topic you choose in your pursuit of personal success.

One of the easiest ways to learn how to do something is to find someone who knows how to do what you want to learn and ask them to teach you. This makes it so much easier than having to figure it out by yourself.

Principle 15: You Have to Be an Avid Learner. You must be an avid learner. One way to do that is to accept that the BIGGER your bookshelves, with books you have actually read, the BIGGER your potential.

Notes

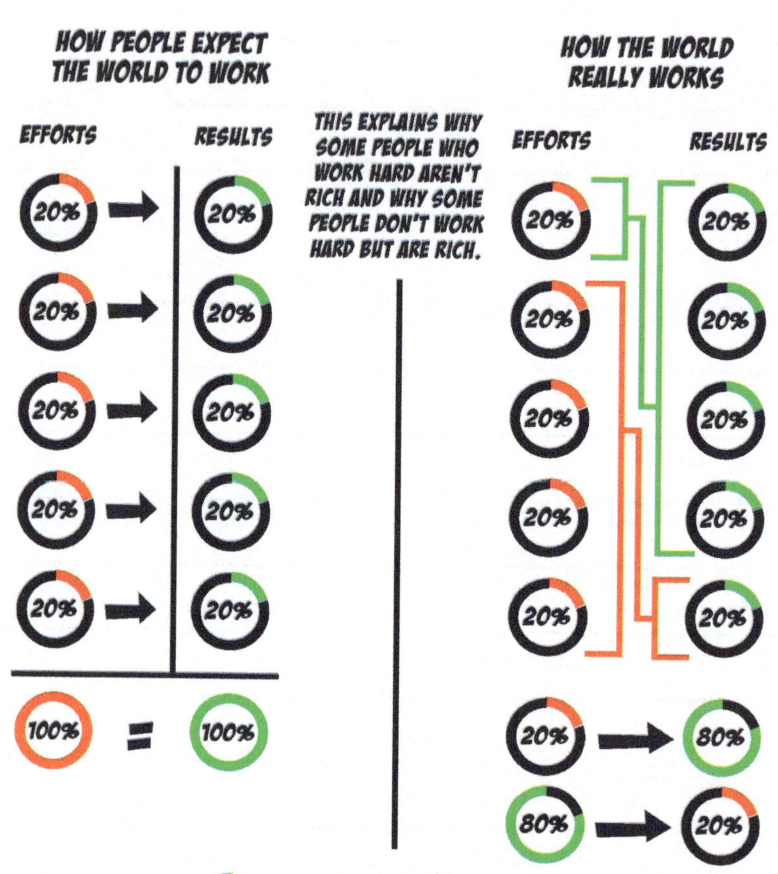

SO DO MORE OF THE 20% WHICH GIVES YOU 80% OF RESULTS, THEN 100% EFFORT GIVES YOU 400% RESULTS!

THE RULE OF 80/20

Chapter 16 The Rule of 80/20

Creatively figure out ways to do things much better with less effort. Spend your time doing what will give you the best results.

The 80/20 Rule is one of the most powerful principles to use once you understand it. If it seems too complicated, work through it and make sure this is one of the ones you really understand.

Other names for the 80/20 Rule are: the Pareto Principle, the Law of the Vital Few, the Principle of Least Effort, and my favorite, the title of Richard Koch's book, "The 80/20 Principle - The Secret to Achieving More, With Less."

Credit for the discovery of the 80/20 Rule goes to an Italian named Vilfredo Pareto, who came up with the idea over one hundred years ago. One day, he was out in his garden weeding around his pea plants. He noticed that from one hundred pea plants, about twenty of the plants produced about eighty percent of the healthy peapods. It fascinated him. He decided to figure out a way to explain it, to validate his discovery that the amount of effort you give to a task is not always equal to the results you achieve.

As he searched around, he began to notice the 80/20 pattern everywhere. Of all of the people he knew, there was a small group he spoke to regularly, what you might call his inner circle of friends. Not because he was unfriendly, but that's how it was – of all of his friends, he spent most of his time with about twenty percent of his friends. Likewise, of all of the clothes he had, there were some clothes that he wore regularly, while some of his clothing was rarely worn. He thought about the roads he traveled in his town going to school, church, and the other places he went. There were lots of roads that he would travel, but some of them were used all of the time, and the others rarely.

It was hard to prove that all of these observations were examples of the 80/20 Rule, but he knew he would figure something out. One da,y he was traveling a road that he normally didn't travel, where there was a beautiful farmhouse, a barn, lots of cattle and acres of land. He had an idea. He talked to the farmer, who owned 3 other farms that were even bigger! It seemed kind of unfair, but he went deeper with his theory. He looked up all of the land owners in Italy and he found that roughly 80% of the land in Italy was owned by 20% of the people. He began to inquire about land ownership in other countries and found that while the number is not always 80/20, these other countries had similar skewed ownership of the land in Italy. Roughly 20% of the people owned roughly 80% of the land.

Later in life, when you have responsibilities and you have to make money to pay bills, the 80/20 Rule will be the most valuable to you. It will benefit you greatly to understand it now though.

Here is how you can apply the 80/20 Rule in your life now, even as a kid.

Look at my case. I've written the book you are now reading. What was more valuable to me, watching TV or writing these words for you to read? Or think of the golfer who wants to go pro; which investment of time is more valuable to his or her goals, taking practice swings with a foam golf ball, or training with a coach hitting real balls on a golf course? To the student, what makes more sense, finishing the paper due the next day that is 25% of your grade, or finishing your homework due in 3 days?

I have noticed with my own traditional business that even though we give all of our customers equal and quality service, there are customers who are much more valuable than others. We strive to gain more customers that are more valuable and eliminate those who are less valuable.

I recently read a report from Oxfam International that said in 2017, there were forty-two billionaires who owned as much as the poorest 50% of the world's population, or 3.7 billion people. If we all have equal time to do things, how is it that these forty-two people control such a vast amount of wealth? There is no doubt that there are people who have worked much harder; but it is not how hard you work, it is the value of what you do that gives the greatest results.

As your understanding of the 80/20 Rule deepens, you will begin to understand that there are other rules within this rule. Examples include the 16x rule, the 1/20 rule, the 5/50 rule, the 1/99 rule, but for now just realize that 50% of effort won't give you 50% of results. It is not always 80/20, it can be 64/36, or 75/25, or 84/16; in each of these examples, we realize that our efforts will not always equal our results.

Stated once again, this is one of the most important principles you can learn. There is a way to achieve way more with less effort. By learning all of the principles in this book and doing outside reading, you will understand how the 80/20 Rule is affecting your success.

Principle 16: The Rule of 80/20. Identify the most valuable things that give you the best results for your effort, then do more of them. Find the things you do that are not the best use of your time, find others to do them, or quit doing them altogether. It is that simple.

1. ASK = MAYBE YES?
MAYBE NO?

2. DON'T ASK = NO (GUARANTEED NO!)

YOU CANNOT GET A YES BY NOT ASKING.

YOU HAVE TO ASK

Chapter 17 You Have to Ask

Don't be afraid to ask for what you want. The worst someone can say is no, but they might say yes. If you do not ask, the answer is always no. Go ahead and ask, you have more to lose by not asking.

If you don't ask for what you want, you will lessen your chances for success. Along the journey to achieving your goals and dreams, you will need advice or help from others. If you need help or guidance, ask for it; if you don't ask, the answer is no. If you do ask, the answer might be yes. What do you have to lose, the worst someone can say is no?

There is no need to re-invent the wheel, which means that if there is a way to do what you want to do, there is usually somebody who has done it. I'll share a hidden secret with you: Most of the time, people who accomplish great things are usually willing to share their experience with others. BUT YOU MUST ASK THEM!

Even famous, successful people, who may not be available to you, can teach you. There is more than likely a treasure of information about them online. Ask Google, and you will find interviews, biographies, articles, videos, and more from which you can learn. Check the library or bookstore for a biography about the person in whom you are interested.

But, this isn't just true for big ideas and famous people. Don't be afraid to ask about small things that others may know. Maybe you just want a hard-boiled egg, and you have never boiled an egg. Ask your mom or grandmother how to do it. Of course, you can just try it and see if you could figure it out, but if you can ask to make your life easier, you should do it.

This ask thing should not be used just to be lazy. Don't just ask your mom to get you a glass of milk if she is sitting next to you on the couch. Or just randomly ask for things without offering anything of value in return.

Most things in life are a negotiation. If you need or want something, there is a usually a way to get it; you just have to get creative and perhaps offer something in return? By asking, you then can figure out what you need to do to make it work.

"Ask and you shall receive" is a quote from the Christian Bible that people use when they encourage others to go after what they want. It works for many things. For example, you may need some weights to work out, but you don't have the money. There may be a friend, family member, or even neighbor who has a bunch of weights that you could use. Sometimes, they may even want to get rid of them and were even considering throwing them away. By asking about them and explaining your need, you may find that you are doing them a favor by taking them! Or you might be able to negotiate with the neighbor to work for them by cleaning their car, cutting their grass, or making payments to them.

Principle 17: You Have to Ask. There is usually a way to work out most things that you need on the path to your goals and dreams. Sometimes, you must get creative to find the solution. Most of all, you need to ASK!

Notes

AVERAGE/GOOD:

GOLFER, PIANIST,
ARTIST, STUDENT,
WORKER, ETC.

5,000 OR LESS HOURS

- HAVE FUN
-DON'T QUIT DAY JOB
- KEEP FOCUSED PRACTICING

5,000-10,000 FOCUSED HOURS OF PRACTICED

- MAKE $ AT IT
- BREAK RECORDS
- INNOVATE
- MAKE THE RULES

THE PRACTICE OF 10,000 HOURS

Chapter 18. The Practice of 10,000 Hours

The practice of 10,000 hours is like that old saying, "Practice makes perfect". Anything you do requires experience and practice. Logic says the more times you do something, the better you get at it. Practice is focused action to get better at an activity.

The idea of practicing something for 10,000 hours to master it comes from Malcolm Gladwell's book, "Outliers: The Story of Success". While studying very successful people, he noticed that one thing they had in common was not a tremendous amount of talent, but that they had put in at least 10,000 hours of diligent practice toward their mastery.

While he found that there were people who were really good at what they did, what stood out is that those who reached the top of their game had usually put in twice as much practice as the others.

It's simple; you must put in the time. If you are not any good after trying a few times, don't get upset or think that you cannot do what you love and really want to do. After 10,000 hours of practice, you can be really good at just about anything.

If you are kid and you are reading this, then you have lots of time to work on practicing for 10,000 hours. The beautiful thing is that now is when you should put in the time because when you grow up, you have to earn a living. It becomes harder to find time to practice toward mastery. As a kid, you will have more time available since you don't have to earn a living yet. Take the time now to research ideas, read books, and talk to successful people. Consistently practice what you want to master.

Let me be really clear—it is not enough to just practice. You must have focused, structured, and well-thought-out practice. What if you practice, but practice the wrong things? What if you wanted to be really good at baseball, but you only practiced hitting? Your 10,000 hours wouldn't get you far if you weren't also good at catching and throwing the ball well.

I once had a friend who really impressed me. His business trained people in big companies on how to achieve their goals and be more valuable to their company. I wanted to do something similar to what he did. I asked him how he did it. He told me he read nearly 500 books to learn how to help people achieve their goals. After reading so many books on this subject, they all started to sound familiar; at that point, he realized he could write his own book and create his own training program. His advice was to figure out what I wanted to do, read 500 books about it, then I would be an expert. I took his advice; I've made it a point to read at least one book per week, sometimes more. Through this form of practice, I've read hundreds of books over the past 20 years, and like my friend, I've created a similar training system, except for kids!

Principle 18: The Practice of 10,000 Hours. The point is—you need to practice, you need to learn, you need to put in your time. By starting when you are young, you have more time to put in your 10,000 hours. Just remember, it is not enough to just practice and put in time, you must use your time wisely. And remember, just because you might be too short to be a basketball superstar, you can still get really good and have a lot of fun!

Notes

+

+

A PERSON WITH A GOOD ATTITUDE WILL USUALLY ALWAYS BE CHOSEN OVER A PERSON WITH A BAD ATTITUDE.

+

+

SOMETIMES A PERSON WITH LESS SKILL AND A GOOD ATTITUDE WILL BE CHOSEN OVER A PERSON WITH MORE SKILL AND A BAD ATTITUDE.

SUCCESS IS MORE ABOUT ATTITUDE THAN KNOWLEDGE

Chapter 19 Success Is More About Attitude Than Knowledge

Having a positive attitude while being an expert will take you farther in life than just being an expert in something! To understand this one concept and practice it will increase your chances of success immensely.

Having a good attitude will give you a tremendous edge in life. Attitude is how you choose to think about people, things, and circumstances, then how you act according to the situation.

Having a good attitude comes down to being positive, happy and grateful vs. being negative, unhappy, and ungrateful. People tend to be naturally drawn toward people they like and away from those they don't like. Try this experiment. The next time you are in public, go out of your way to make eye contact and smile at people you encounter. If you walk around with an angry scowl, people will look away and avoid you. Project a positive image always.

For example, there might have been a time when a teacher had to choose between two students for a special program. If two students have equal qualifications, the teacher would choose the student that they felt had the better attitude about life. Teachers understand that while grades and IQ are especially important, attitude is an even better indicator of who will be successful.

Here are some other examples:

1. Studies have shown that people will buy inferior products that cost more from people with good attitudes whom they like and trust more over people with overall better products but whom

they didn't like. That should be enough for anyone to develop a great attitude.

2. Think of attitude like the weather. What would be a better day to have your birthday party outside? A nice beautiful day with perfect blue skies, comfortable temperature, and mild breeze, or a cloudy, rainy, cold, windy and dreary day? You and your friends would not enjoy bad weather for your birthday party, and neither would you enjoy being with friends who have dreary attitudes. Don't bring bad weather into your life with a bad attitude.

3. If you have a dog, you can relate to this example. Would you rather play with a dog that comes up wagging their tail, full of joy, wanting to play, or a mean dog barking and growling at you with their teeth showing? Nobody likes playing with a mean dog. You stay away so you don't get bitten! The same is true in life. If given a choice, people will choose the person with the good attitude.

In life, especially in the workforce, people who have good attitudes are more desirable to be around, more likely to be hired, and more often considered for opportunities. It's the same on sports teams, the friends you have, and other relationships.

Principle 19: Success Is More About Attitude Than Knowledge. Your attitude is more important than your knowledge when it comes to being successful. Some people naturally have a good attitude, but not everyone does. Commit to learning how to have a good attitude or strengthening your good attitude. Be positive, happy, grateful, and full of energy about life. It will propel you a lot further than you will get with only your good looks and smart brain.

Notes

NEGATIVE/ PESSIMISM

WILL ALWAYS SEE THE BAD WEATHER

POSITIVE/ OPTIMISM

WILL ALWAYS SEE THE GOOD WEATHER

HAVE A POSITIVE VIEW OF THE WORLD

Chapter 20 Have a Positive View of The World

We are living in two different worlds. One of them attracts bad, one of them attracts good. It is your job to be positive and an optimist so your life attracts more good things. You attract what you think, so think good thoughts!

The two worlds we live in are the positive world, where your attitude is called optimism, or the negative world where your attitude is called pessimism. You must choose which world you will live in.

This principle has everything to do with the way you think, which directly affects your attitude. Which world you choose to be a part of will have a direct impact on the way you see the world and how others see and relate to you. Some will tell you that how you choose to think about your situations, whether positive or negative, can affect your health and overall well-being.

One of the best ways to understand the difference between being positive or negative is the classic water in the glass example. Picture a glass that is filled to the mid-point with water. Is that glass half full or half empty? A positive person would say it was half full, which is considered the optimistic view; a negative person would say it was half empty, which is considered the pessimistic view.

By choosing to be positive, you are considered an optimist. An optimist is someone who sees things in the world as good. There will always be good and bad things in your life. To be a positive person is to choose to focus your thoughts on the good things and find something positive about the bad ones.

For the purpose of accomplishing your goals and dreams, being a positive person who focuses on the good in life is a requirement.

You will learn to see anything negative or bad as temporary, a learning lesson, and something that will work itself out. You will automatically be confident that things will work out in your favor, and that life will be good for you. You will believe that someday your goals and dreams will work out, and you will be happy as you are working toward them.

As an optimist, you understand that things could always be much worse than they are, and you are always grateful they are not.

If you are one of the unlucky ones who choose to be negative, you would be considered a pessimist. A pessimist is a person who finds the negative in any situation. Instead of focusing on the positive and good things in life, they will focus on what is not good.

Being a negative person will have you always looking for reasons why things won't work out, why things are bad ideas, seeing fault with people, doubting your abilities and the abilities of others. By thinking this way, it can be compared to growing a dark rain cloud in your mind that puts out the fire of your goals and dreams.

Making excuses about why an idea or a dream won't work is not productive. Be an optimist who figures out you can make it work. There will be disappointments where things are not going to work, and you are not happy. In those times, you must think about them in the best possible way and seek out the lesson to learn or the positive aspect that is hiding in the situation.

Principle 20: Have a Positive View of the World. Even if you learn all of the principles in this book, if you don't have a positive view of the world and your abilities to achieve your dreams, you are doomed to have a storm cloud follow you around life. It is your job to attract good things by practicing a positive attitude.

Notes

DON'T DO THE 3 C'S

Chapter 21 Don't Do The 3 C's

Don't Criticize, Condemn or Complain. These habits are equally toxic to success. They are destructive, so they have no place in helping you to achieve your goals. You will have the best luck in life staying away from these three C's.

Criticizing, condemning, or complaining comes down to this truth. No one wants to hear your negativity, so keep it to yourself.

To criticize is to find fault with other people or things. To condemn is to blame people and show your complete disapproval. To complain is to whine and be annoyed with a person or thing.

The human mind is like a garden that, when praised, complimented, and supported, will grow beautiful plants; but when blamed, disapproved, and proven wrong, will shrivel up and die.

People are slow to admit they are wrong. To be told or to be proven wrong is a type of criticism that makes others feel bad about themselves and doesn't win you any awards. It can cause resentment from the person and make them feel they must justify themselves. Once they feel that way, you will not win them to your way of thinking. Whatever negativity you have given to someone will rebound back to you by their resentment.

Pride is at the root of such feelings. People want to feel special, smart, accomplished, or important. What if you were a carpenter who was building a beautiful home? Someone comes to you and says, "That's not a nice home, you are doing that wrong. I wouldn't have done it like that." It doesn't make you very happy, does it? In your mind, you are doing the best you can and will resent anybody who tries to tear down your home with their criticism. You have put in a lot of time and effort. Instead of thinking, "Thanks, I'm so glad you mentioned that", you will be thinking, "How dare you? Who do you think you are?" even if you, the carpenter, are building the house completely wrong.

We are not perfect; everyone has their faults and problems. Instead of pointing out the faults of others, we should be working on fixing our own problems.

If you want to help the carpenter build a beautiful home, tell him or her something positive to help build their pride. Anything but constructive, positive reinforcement should be prohibited.

If judgement is necessary, do it in a way that is helpful and constructive, in a way that will not damage the precious pride of others. We are all emotional beings who thrive off words of encouragement and praise.

Remember the example of the carpenter next time you want to offer someone negativity. Offer something that will benefit them, even if it is just some positive words.

Principle 21: Don't do the Three C's. Don't be known as the person who Criticizes, Condemns or Complains. No one wants to hear your negative judgements, so if you can't say something good, don't say anything at all.

Notes

COMPUTER

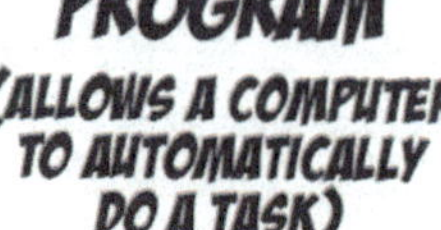

YOUR MIND
(COMPUTER)

HABITS
(PROGRAM)
ALLOW YOU TO
AUTOMATICALLY
DO A TASK

JUST LIKE YOU CAN CHANGE A PROGRAM IN A COMPUTER, YOU CAN CHANGE YOUR HABITS!

Chapter 22 Habits

Habits are those little things that we do so many times, over and over, that they become natural, and you don't even have to think about them. Good habits are what will help you to stay consistent as you work toward your goals and dreams.

Once you do something enough times, it becomes a habit and sometimes it becomes hard to stop. Our habits can be helpful, like eating lots of fruits and veggies. They can be neutral like taking a shower every morning at the same time. Some habits are destructive, such as smoking or eating too much sugary food.

Your brain is like a computer, and your habits can be compared to computer programs. You will automatically do certain things based on habit, because the consistent repetition has created a program in your brain, which means habits can be difficult to break.

The key is to understand which habits are bad, and then figure out how to change them. It may take some major effort at first, but as you consistently keep doing something that is not a habit, it will gradually become a habit. There have been many studies done on forming new habits. The rule everyone always talks about is that it takes 21 days to form a new habit. Some habits may take much longer to create.

Sometimes, people want to change everything in their life. They try to create a bunch of new habits at once. This is EXTREMELY hard to do, and not recommended. It is best to start with creating one new habit at a time, trading a bad habit for the new good one that you are trying to create.

The military uses the habit of keeping your shoes shined, your bed made, and reporting for early morning formations as part of their overall plan of having highly trained soldiers ready for battle. The habits are simple, yet those small habits lead to attention to detail in their focus in battle and training.

A good example is a habit I developed when writing this book. I would try to write when I could, but usually, my regular habits got in the way of my writing. I would have work-related things get in the way, I would want to do cool stuff with my son, and I would take trips. In other words, I was drawn toward my existing habits that did not include writing my book. Then, I made a commitment to develop a new habit that I could do consistently. I started going to bed at 9:30 p.m. instead of at random times. I would get out of be at 5:30 a.m. and immediately go to the computer to write a chapter of the book. I would stay at it until I had written at least 500 words.

Principle 22: Habits. Habits must be cultivated. When going after your goals and dreams, there is a lot of hard work and things you must do to make them happen. Habits are the structure of how your mind helps you create a program for how you will achieve them.

Notes

USE THE LAW OF 80% 20% TO FIGURE OUT WHAT YOUR MOST IMPORTANT THING IS THAT WILL GIVE YOU THE BEST RESULTS, AND DO THAT THING FIRST.

1. MOST IMPORTANT
2. IMPORTANT
3. NEEDED
4. NOT NEEDED NOW
5. LOWEST VALUE

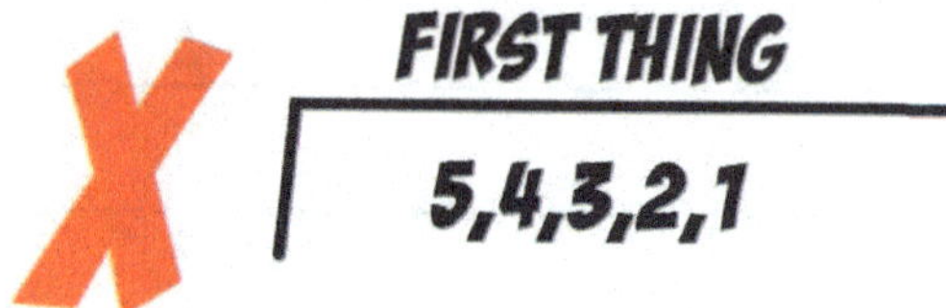

DO THE MOST IMPORTANT THING FIRST

Chapter 23 Do the Most Important Thing First

Every day you wake up and begin again with a fresh start. You have things that you must do, things you want to do and things you don't want to do. It is to your most advantage to take care of the most important thing first.

Imagine that you have a chance to go to the waterpark for a big birthday party that all of your friends are going to in the afternoon, as long as your room is clean. Why not get it clean in the morning, first thing, before you watch television, play on the internet, or skateboard? It is your most important thing to do. You can't miss all of that fun!

When you get home from school, you know there are a million things that you can do, but you have homework that must be done. Do it first if it's the most important thing to do. That way, your important thing is out of the way, and you are free to do whatever you want.

How will this habit help as you get older and gain the responsibilities of an adult? Once you are in college, the workforce, or in business, doing the most important thing first will keep you always moving forward. It is easy to slack off or do a bunch of easy, not so important things and waste time in the process.

The 80/20 Rule states that 20% of your effort leads to 80% of your results; by doing your most important tasks first thing each day, you are getting the most results for your efforts. If you do that one important first task, and slack off for the rest of the day, you will be doing WAY better than if you just focused on less important tasks.

When you are on a mission of accomplishing your goals and dreams, there is the big picture that is your end result. But it's the little steps that lead to achieving your end result. Now, realize you take steps one at a time. If you try to take 2 steps at once, you are just hopping and not taking steps. It is important to focus on doing the most important step first, then the next most important, and so on.

You cannot run to the left and right at the same time. You have to choose one way to go. The same is true with the steps to achieving your goals. There may be two or three equally important things that will get you tremendous results. Focus on ONE of them until it is complete, then focus on the next one; otherwise, you risk none of them getting done.

If you take a step each day that leads toward your goals and dreams, what do you think happens? Each day, you are moving in the right direction by doing the most important thing first!

Principle 23: Do the Most Important Thing First. Start your day by doing the most important thing first. Make sure you begin your day by doing the one important thing that will give you the maximum benefit and results first. Don't try to do more than that one thing until it is complete, then you can move on to the next thing. By doing this, you will be moving your plans forward one day at a time and not wasting your efforts on things that are less important.

Notes

FIRST IMPRESSIONS

EQUAL
QUALIFICATIONS

EQUAL
QUALIFICATIONS

BE PRESENTABLE AND ON TIME

Chapter 24 Be Presentable and On Time

In life, people instantly judge others in a variety of ways. There is nothing you can do about snap judgements except do your best to make the best impression, to look and act your best, and to show up when you say you will. These habits will give you an instant edge.

The world is highly judgmental, especially upon a first meeting. The first time you meet someone new, especially if it's for something important to you—such as applying for a job, finding a mentor, qualifying for a special program, or making a team, the first impression you make on the person you are meeting is extremely important because you can't get a "re-do".

First impressions are extremely valuable to you; do your best to make the best first impression possible by dressing neatly, acting positively and showing up ON TIME!

People will make judgements about you in a split second. Unfortunately, this first judgement is hard to break once it is made. By not taking advantage of this first opportunity, you are not maximizing your total potential.

To be neatly dressed, with clean hair neatly arranged, and showing up on time are all key. You will be judged on those things before you even say one word, or before someone even sees your qualifications. Start swearing, and your stock automatically goes way down too.

This snap judgement is not fair. It can be traced back thousands of years when humans had to make quick decisions based on the need to survive. In our time, these snap judgements are not as important as they were for our ancestors, but they are still part of how our brains work.

The impression your appearance leaves goes beyond the first meeting. It signals to the world that you are confident, you are important, you are somebody. It also mentally works in your favor. It makes YOU feel confident and important. You can make yourself feel that way even if you are having a bad day, just by acting like someone who is confident and important.

When someone chooses to meet with you, they are giving up their time. People's time is valuable because you can't just get more of it. Some professional people like lawyers or doctors may charge hundreds of dollars per hour! By not being on time, you send a message to the other party that you don't care about them because you don't care about their time.

When two equally qualified candidates are being considered for something like a job, if one candidate is well dressed, clean cut and on time, they will generally have a better chance of being chosen than the one who is not dressed as well or shows up late. There are many times, the well dressed, on time, less qualified candidate will be chosen because they have put in the effort to respect themselves and other people.

Principle 24: Be Presentable and Show Up on Time. Take these simple principles to heart. Being well kept and showing up on time leads you to become more valuable to yourself and others.

Notes

EAT UNHEALTHY

DON'T EXCERCISE

LACK OF WATER

EAT HEALTHY

EXCERCISE

DRINK LOTS OF WATER

EAT HEALTHY, EXCERCISE, DRINK LOTS OF WATER!

Chapter 25 Eat Healthy, Exercise, and Drink Lots of Water

Hippocrates, an ancient Greek who is considered the Father of Medicine, said, "Let food be thy medicine, and medicine be thy food." In today's terms, the saying, "You are what you eat" means the same thing.

You only get one body, and it thrives under the right circumstances. Under the wrong circumstances, it becomes damaged, attracts disease, and will lack energy.

The fortunate thing is that we are more in control of our health and well-being than you might think. I've written this chapter because of a personal health issue that I experienced. It is one of the main reasons why you are reading this book in the first place.

When you are young, it is difficult to realize that without your health and energy, nothing else matters. There are kids who are very familiar with how poor health affects their life if they or a family member have a serious illness. The important lesson is that to achieve your goals and dreams in life, you must give your body the best chance for success by giving it more of what it needs, and less of what it does not need.

What I liked to do was drink lots of coffee with way too much sugar. I liked to go to fast food restaurants every day for my breakfast and lunch. I would eat lots of candy and drink sugary soda every day. I would eat all kinds of processed foods like snacks, chips, cookies, anything that comes in a package. I would eat lots of fried food, hot dogs, and have dinner in restaurants. I was on a high sugar, fast food, processed food diet, and then one day it happened.

I started to have problems with my stomach. It started to get so bad that I couldn't do anything and had no energy. I couldn't even work!

I went to the doctor and he put me on all kinds of medicine that wasn't working. What was happening is that my immune system was attacking my body. My energy was low. My eyes and skin were turning gray. I kept getting sicker, and I lost 1/3 of my total body weight before I figured out what I was going to do.

My coach told me that I needed to change my diet, that changing my diet was my only hope. I listened, and I made the change! I eliminated sugar, gluten, fast food, fried food, processed food, coffee, and carbonated drinks immediately. I began to eat all natural and drink lots of water.

There was a time I was really discouraged because I still felt really sick. Then, a funny thing happened. After a few months of healthy eating, my body started to show signs of healing, and I started feeling better. Once I saw a little hope, I knew I was doing the right thing.

I learned from experience just how important what you eat affects how you feel and function. I went from being unable to work, unable to make my goals and dreams come true to where I am now. If you are reading this, it means it worked; my dreams are coming true, and the changes I made were very important for my goals and dreams.

As I was going through my health issues, I studied many things about health (Remember, I told you that to master something, you must read lots of books about it!). It seems there were lots of people who were very ill, but their health improved when they changed their diet and started exercising.

My recommendation to you is this: Practice eating only real foods, drinking lots of water, and exercise daily. By real foods, I mean foods that are not processed and wrapped in a package but prepared from fresh ingredients. Instead of treating illnesses and disease, try to prevent them whenever possible. Eating natural foods, drinking lots of water, and exercising daily are habits that support my recommendation.

Principle 25: Eat Healthy, Exercise, and Drink Lots of Water. Don't wait to become sick, or out of shape with no energy. Take a preventative approach to your health. Don't risk going through what I did, or even worse. Instead, choose to eat fresh fruits and veggies every day, drink lots of water, and exercise. A life full of energy is worth it, and your goals and dreams depend on it!

AQUACULTURE - GROW FISH IN A FARM

WASTE? WHAT TO DO WITH IT?
*NEED TO GET RID OF IT

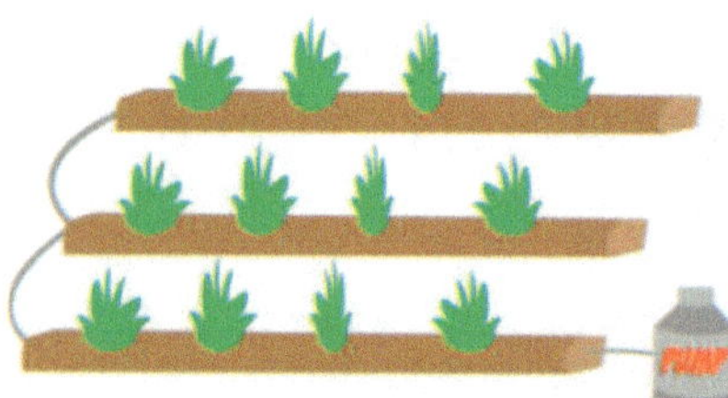

HYDROPONICS - GROW FOOD IN WATER

FERTILIZER?
*NEED TO ADD NUTRIENTS

Chapter 26. WIN/WIN

In a negotiation, look for ways to benefit everyone. Sometimes, a win/ win will yield far better results than if you tried to get everything for yourself.

Often times, when one person wins, the idea is that the other person loses in a negotiation. It doesn't always have to be that way.

With creative thinking, everyone can benefit from the final solution. Don't let fear or impatience prevent you from looking for that creative way for everyone to win in a situation.

The best example I know of a win/ win is with aquaponics. Aquaponics is a farming technique that combines growing fish and growing vegetables together.

It is the blending of two industries to create a new and better alternative.

Aquaculture is the technique used to farm fish. People grow the fish in water holding areas. There is a problem removing the waste from the water. Because the fish are not in a natural lake or pond that gets fresh water regularly, the waste can build up. If the waste gets too bad, the fish could be poisoned by their own waste, so there needs to be really good filters to try to clean the water. Cleaning the water in aquaculture is a BIG problem!

Hydroponics is growing vegetables in water without soil. Water is running through a closed system that keeps the plant's roots in water and not soil. Since most things need water to grow, this technique has incredibly good results. The problem with hydroponics is that you must KEEP adding fertilizer to the system.

By combining aquaculture and hydroponics, aquaponics creates a win/ win situation. Fish waste becomes the fertilizer for the hydroponics, and the hydroponics becomes the filter for the aquaculture. Not only that, but there is like 90% less water use, no fertilizer and pesticide. The plants thrive in aquaponics systems, the crops grow faster, and the systems use much less land. Big WIN / WIN!

By looking for the win/ win in your life circumstances, you will be able to get more cooperation from other people and come up with better solutions than if someone always has to lose.

Principle 26: WIN / WIN. Get better results for both parties by thinking of creative solutions where each party benefits. Remember how fish and plants each benefited from aquaponics—how can you apply that example to your situation?

Notes

FOCUS: PICK A GOAL OR DREAM AND STICK WITH IT UNTIL THE END.

DISCIPLINE: RULES OR HOW YOU ACT WHILE GOING AFTER YOUR DREAMS AND GOALS

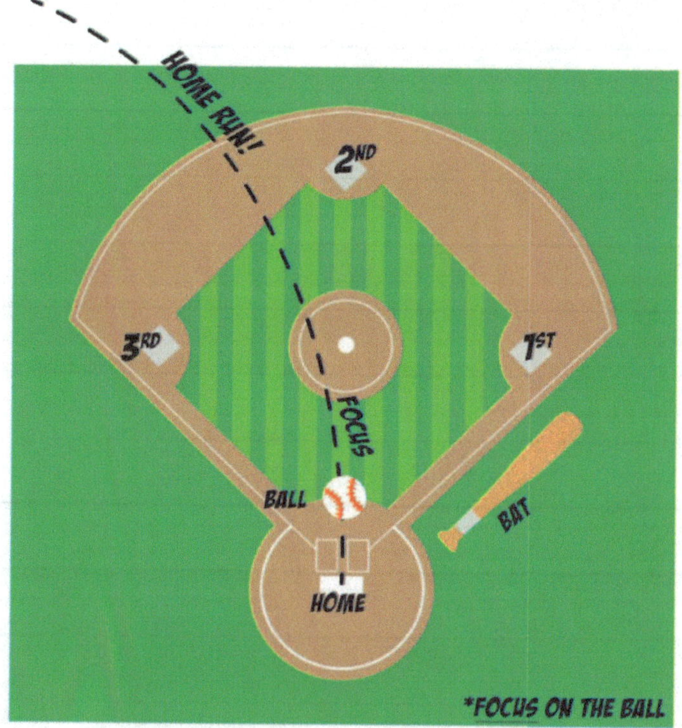

HAVE FOCUS AND DISCIPLINE

Chapter 27. Have Focus and Discipline

Sometimes, with major goals and dreams, you have to put in a lot of hard work for a long time before you see any results. That is where discipline and focus come in.

Do you have any idea how many balls a professional golfer hits before they become pro? I estimate millions. How many hours of time does that take? Walking the golf courses, training, working with coaches, becoming good at golf, all of these steps take a lot of effort—years and years of it.

Perhaps, you want to be a doctor? After four years of college, and four years of medical school, which are both very time consuming and not easy to get through, a typical doctor could spend another three to seven years in residency. That means they are in a clinical setting, like a hospital, not making very much money, and working grueling hours.

Doctors spend years going through the medical studies program before they ever make any money. They need tremendous discipline and focus to stay with it instead of going out and finding a job to pay for their increasing schooling costs.

Focus is being able to pick the end result of your goal and dream and stick with it until you achieve that end. As you can see, with major aspirations, there may be years of effort before you achieve your goal. There may be barriers that try to prevent you from getting to the end. Focusing on the end goal is what will get you through these times.

A lack of focus means you could go from one idea to the next without ever really accomplishing anything.

Discipline is the rule of how you act while going after your goals and dreams. It is using all of the things found in this book to your advantage. It is the glue that keeps it all together. It is the guideline that keeps you going straight on the road to your success when you want to take a right or a left. When you chose to work on your goals instead of doing other fun things—that is discipline. Not to say you can't have fun. You have to be happy, and NEED TO TAKE TIME OUT FOR PLEASURE AND FUN STUFF!

An example of discipline is always focusing on the most important thing you have to do first toward achieving your goal when you start your day instead of some random thing you could be doing. Another would be to practice a skill every day for at least an hour. Making it a habit to read for an hour a day to learn what it takes to accomplish your goals and dreams takes discipline.

If you were on a diet, it would take discipline to always eat the right type of food instead of junk food. Your focus would be to lose weight, and be healthy, but your discipline would be that rule of not eating the wrong food.

Principle 27: Have Focus and Discipline. Focus is what you direct toward your end result, and discipline is the set of rules you give yourself on the road to attaining your end result.

Notes

FIXED MINDSET
I'M PERFECT. I'M SMART.
BECAUSE I'M PERFECT & SMART, I DON'T MAKE MISTAKES
I MADE A MISTAKE!?
I BETTER NOT DO ANYTHING OUT OF MY COMFORT ZONE SO I DON'T MAKE ANY MORE MISTAKES.
GROWTH MINDSET
I CAN LEARN ANYTHING!
I MADE A MISTAKE. I'LL LEARN FROM IT.
NOW, I CAN TRY NEW THINGS WITHOUT FEAR OF MESSING UP!
FIXED MINDSET VS. GROWTH MINDSET

Chapter 28 Fixed Mindset Vs. Growth Mindset

This is all about not being afraid to make mistakes and knowing that you can learn from them. It is OK to make mistakes, just don't keep making the same ones! Don't fear mistakes by not acting.

Fixed mindset and growth mindset are two different ways of thinking about things that will make a big difference in your journey to success. A fixed mindset person believes that you are gifted from birth, and the growth mindset person believes that you can practice, learn, and gain experience to become gifted.

Having a fixed mindset will limit your ability to master whatever subject you want to pursue. Here is why: Fixed mindset people believe that they are born either smart or not so smart; that they have to be perfect and do everything right the first time. They go through great efforts to be right and never be wrong. They are always looking for ways of validating how smart or good they are. They believe in fixed traits, that what you have is all you will ever have, as far as knowledge, talent and skills are concerned. Trying and wanting to appear better than others, they are quick to correct others or point out when someone is wrong.

This approach is very limiting and causes people to avoid trying to attempt something they think is difficult, or avoid taking risks, for fear of being inadequate in their mind or in front of others.

A fixed mindset is inferior to a growth mindset because you can develop skills, you can develop intelligence, and you can develop knowledge.

By approaching your dreams and goals with a growth mindset, you understand that if you are diligent in your practice and diligent in learning, you will grow your skills and knowledge. You are not stuck with the knowledge and abilities you had when you were born.

There are many examples of wildly successful people who are naturally considered really smart or gifted with intelligence. Most of the time, these people are no smarter than we are. They started out life with the same knowledge and abilities. What drove their success and created the appearance of being gifted is that they put more time and effort into their endeavors.

Here is a great example to explain someone with a growth mindset. How much do you know about Thomas Edison, who is credited for inventing the lightbulb? When the lightbulb was invented, was it an "AH HA!" moment? It was a moment in time when a good idea came to fruition. It is the lightbulb moment that is always talked about when someone has a good idea. It's a stroke of genius. The symbol of the lightbulb appearing over someone's head suggests they are having a good idea and I bet you have seen it in cartoons.

But, in fact, Thomas Edison had a staff of over two dozen intelligent people working for him in a fully equipped, state-of-the-art lab. His, "AH HA!" moment came after thousands of failures!

A genius, also called a prodigy, is born with a high IQ and they can do extraordinary things that normal people must learn and practice to become expert at. Being born a genius is the exception, an anomaly.

We can be like them, but we have to work for it! You, I, or anyone can develop their genius. It comes by effort. Most people will try something a few times and give up. Geniuses like Thomas Edison will try 10,000 times until they figure it out. They will fail, they will have to learn new things, they will enlist help, but their genius comes because they put in the work and weren't afraid of making mistakes.

A growth mindset person realizes that it is ok to make mistakes. They learn from and try not to repeat them. They also realize they can learn from the mistakes of others and strive to avoid making the same ones that others have made. You learn from your own mistakes, but you also must learn what has worked and not worked for others and learn from them.

Principle 28: Fixed Mindset vs. Growth Mindset. Fixed mindset vs. growth mindset will show you that you can also become a genius! You just have to work toward it more than someone born “a genius”.

EMPLOYEE: IS WILLING TO WASH CARS FOR $10 PER HOUR FOR A COMPANY. WASHES 10 CARS IN A WEEK AND MAKES $150. HAS NO RISK OR EXPENSES.

SELF EMPLOYED: WASHES CARS FOR $40 EACH, IT TAKES 1.5 HOURS EACH. DOES 10 CARS IN A WEEK BY SELF AND MAKES $400 MINUS EXPENSES.

ENTREPRENEUR: PAYS EMPLOYEE $10 PER HOUR TO WASH CARS IN 1.5 HOURS EACH. ENTREPRENEUR MAKES $25 MINUS EXPENSES. EMPLOYEE MAKES $15. BY WASHING 10 CARS IN A WEEK THE ENTREPRENEUR MAKES $250 MINUS EXPENSES.
*** ENTREPRENEUR IS FREE TO GET AS MANY EMPLOYEES AND CARS TO WASH AS THEY PLEASE.
*** ENTREPRENEUR MAKES MONEY FROM CREATING A SYSTEM, NOT WORKING FOR AN HOURLY WAGE.

ENTREPRENEURSHIP IS KEY!

Chapter 29 Entrepreneurship Is Key

Entrepreneurship is a secret that is not taught in schools. Entrepreneurship is the act of setting up a business to create a profit. There is risk of failure and losing all of your money, but there is also the possibility of making it BIG!

It's hard for kids to find paying jobs. Sometimes, the local grocery or hardware store will hire fifteen-year-old kids, but what about ten or eleven-year-old kids? A kid might get lucky and have a family member in business that they can work for, but not everyone has that ability.

The best thing for a kid to do to make some money is to start their own business. Traditionally, kids have started service-related businesses such as lawn care, house cleaning, dog walking, babysitting, and car washing. When I was a kid, I mowed lawns and shoveled snow. Out of all of my childhood friends, I was always the kid with the money, which allowed me to buy things like nice bikes, better hockey equipment, and video games.

Today, there are true entrepreneurship opportunities available online, even for kids. There are kids making more money than their parents with their online business. Entrepreneurship is one of the key ways that kids can make money before they are old enough for real jobs.

Some of the ways kids are making money are by doing toy review videos, selling products on Amazon and eBay, and writing/publishing their own books. Some kids have YouTube videos that make a lot of money from advertising. There are even kids blogging. It is truly amazing! If you are a kid who wants to start your own business, online is the way to do it!

Traditionally, kids are taught that the path to success is to get good grades in school, go to college, then get a good job. It is a safe and common way for people to succeed. Here is a comparison of the traditional path to success compared to entrepreneurship:

This is how most kids are taught in school:

Go to elementary school, middle school, and high school to prep for college.

Go to college and get a degree.

Then go on to find a good paying job (Not guaranteed).

Save and invest money towards your retirement, slowly building wealth.

Work at your job until age sixty-five, or when you have enough money to retire.

Retire, hope you live happily ever after and you don't run out of money!

Entrepreneurship works like this:

Find a service or product that people are willing to pay for.

Create a business to sell to those people.

Start bringing in money (Called Cash Flow) until you have built up enough to hire others to help you run the business. These people might be virtual assistants, subcontractors, or regular employees.

As you become more successful, decide how involved you want to be in your business. You may be able to set up systems where the business runs itself because you have hired all the right people, and it requires little or no labor from you.

Or you might be one of those people who love what you do so much that you want to be hands-on and directly involved in steering your company in the direction you want it to go.

Entrepreneurship is a way of thinking about business where even kids can achieve abundant financial results if they have the right idea! Imagine this scenario: It is your job to wash ten cars every weekend. For each car you wash, you will earn $40, or a total of $400. After you pay for supplies, the rest is profit that you can keep.

If you hire other people to do the work, then line up more work, you can make even more money without having to do the actual, "work". In the above example, if your hourly employee at $10 per hour can do one car in 1.5hrs and each car is worth $40, then your take is $25 per car. If they did 10 cars, that total would be $250! Subtract $50 for expenses and you just made $200 having someone else do the work. What's to stop you from hiring a second employee and getting 20 cars to wash making twice the profit not washing any of the cars? Or triple, and so on?

Being an entrepreneur takes work for sure, to get a business started. Even though it sounds great, in the grand scheme of things, most businesses fail. Here's a little secret; we have a plan to fix that! Make sure to follow us, to get on our email list to find out how!

The ultimate goal with entrepreneurship should be to get rich as fast as possible and spend the rest of your life giving it all away, changing the world for the better!

Principle 29: Entrepreneurship is Key! Most of the people who have created tremendous wealth in their lifetimes have been entrepreneurs. If you are too young to find a job with a company, start your own business. You will learn how to run a business, and you may even make money, maybe a lot of money.

ALWAYS HELP OTHERS SUCCEED WHEN YOU CAN

Chapter 30 Always Help Others Succeed When You Can

The first principle in this book, The Golden Rule, discusses that when you throw a boomerang it goes out, then turns and comes back to you. Helping others succeed when you can works in a similar way. If you look out for others, others will look out for you. Sometimes, investing just a short amount of your time can dramatically change someone's life. Another way to say it is that you are paying it forward.

If you think of success as a team effort, you become one of the team members working toward success. By helping to move the team forward, you move yourself forward toward your goal. If the team succeeds, so do you, or if the team fails, each team member individually fails.

I have personally used this concept in my life. There were times when I helped people who could not repay me. I have always looked for situations where a small amount of effort on my part could help others dramatically.

I believe that because I have practiced this principle, it seems that I receive help from others in my own pursuit of success. Sometimes, I receive a little help, other times I received an abundance of help and support. I have come to realize that you get back what you give to others, and by helping others succeed when you can, others help you succeed when they can.

I've thought about why this principle works. The trick is that everyone is always looking for something, whether it's money, help or something else. Because everyone has these needs, there are times when you can help to a point where it harms you or the people you care about. Learn to find the balance of helping where you can without risking your own needs. Worry about your own life, but if you are willing and capable, help where you can.

Think of this: You cannot help someone else pay for their meal when you cannot pay for your own food. You cannot spend all day helping someone else do their homework when yours is not done. Not only do you hurt yourself, you may also hurt others like your family, who count on you to take care of yourself.

Throughout your life, there will be people you will do good things for but will not deserve your kindness. While it may upset you that they don't thank you or show their appreciation, don't let it stop you from helping others, even those who don't seem to deserve it. Sometimes, they are the ones who need the help the most. Over the long term, this principle works.

It's as simple as this: Let's say you put money into a vending machine. It takes your money, then it takes your friend's money. Now, a third person walks up and is about to put in their money. You have to warn them! Warning them of your experience before they put their money into the broken machine makes them better off because you shared your experience.

A business-type example would be for a successful person to mentor and develop your skills to help you become successful. Such an investment of someone's time in you could take years and dedicated efforts.

Principle 30: Always Help Others Succeed When You Can. Whether you help others succeed as a mentor, or by doing the small things for the people in your life, either effort could have major results. When you throw out the boomerang of help, it eventually comes back to you in one form or another.

Notes

"THE STORE IS ON THE RIGHT SIDE OF THE ROAD."

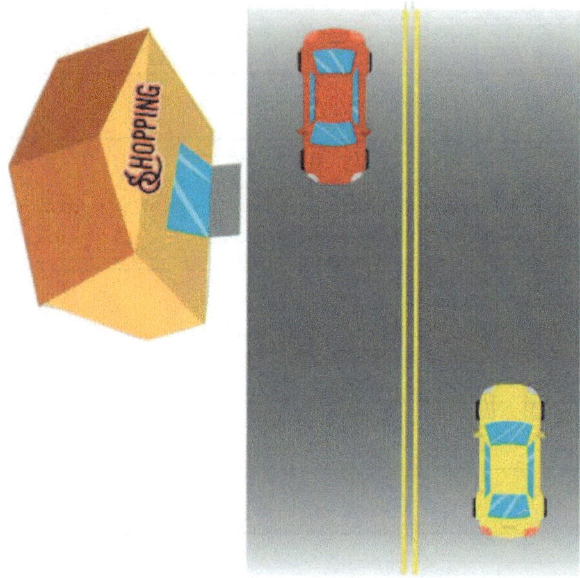

"THE STORE IS ON THE LEFT SIDE OF THE ROAD."

THEIR ANSWERS ARE OPPOSITE, BUT BOTH ARE CORRECT

THE BEST WAY TO WIN AN ARGUEMENT

Chapter 31 The Best Way to Win an Argument

The best way to win an argument is to not argue at all! Arguing should be a big no-no in your life. Arguing can lead to resentment, anger, and frustration by both parties, regardless of who wins or loses the argument.

The problem with arguing is, at the end of it, you don't win an award unless you are a lawyer or on the debate team. Usually, the end of an argument will lead to resentment and the losing party not being convinced of whatever you were arguing about.

To be right or wrong often doesn't make a difference in either person's life. An argument could be defined as two people with a conflicting view trying to prove their knowledge, avoiding being wrong at all costs to avoid hurting their pride.

Sometimes, people will argue because they just want to feel important and smart, but chances are all they are doing is making themselves look the opposite.

Arguing about small things only causes unnecessary stress. Chances are, both parties could be right! Then, arguing becomes a duel for pride. One person wins a little, the other person loses a little, and both parties feel unnecessary stress.

Imagine you are trying to figure out if a destination is on the left side of the road or the right. You ask someone who frequently travels there from the north, and they tell you it's was always on the right. You ask another person who always travel there from the south, and they say it is always on the left. Each person could argue until they are blue in the face about who was right, but in the end, they would both be right and wrong at the same time. It's a matter of perspective, or point of view.

A story that perfectly illustrates this point is about people describing an elephant, but they can't actually see the elephant. It goes like this: Several people are blindfolded and then touch different parts of an elephant. One person can feel the elephant's trunk, the second person feels a leg, the third person feels the tail, the fourth person feels an ear, and the fifth person feels the middle of the elephant's body. Each person would give a different description of what they felt, and they would all be right!

If you feel like you are about to be in an argument because of a difference in opinion, keep your cool and welcome it. For all you know, the other party could be warning you of a major mistake. Accept that they could be right, examine your situation to see if they could be right. Don't risk messing up something because you are too stubborn to consider you could be wrong. When you have a disagreement with someone, look for common ground and make a sincere attempt to understand. But never say, "You are wrong" and risk an argument.

One thing I've noticed about arguments is that sometimes, people will be arguing about the same thing but won't take the time to listen to the other person to realize they agree.

Principle 31: The Best Way to Win an Argument. Try your best not to argue, but to understand. Whether the other party is right or wrong is not the point. The point is that you hear them out to understand their position or perspective. When it comes to arguments, be the bigger person and pour water on the fire before it gets out of hand.

Notes

WHAT YOU SEE

WHAT YOU BOTH SEE WHEN YOU TAKE THE TIME TO SEE THE VIEW POINT OF OTHERS.

*YOU CAN SEE THE WHOLE WORLD

WHAT SOMEONE ELSE SEE'S

BE ABLE TO SEE THINGS FROM OTHER'S VIEWPOINTS

Chapter 32 Be Able to See Things From Other's Viewpoints

Life is one big interaction with other people. Along the way, there will be people who will teach you, people you will teach, and there will be conflicts with others. You can help prevent conflict by considering the other person's viewpoint as you learn from each other.

Everyone has an opinion based on experiences and knowledge that are unique to them.

There are many types of people from all types of backgrounds. Because this is true, you may need some discipline in really trying to understand some people's circumstances. You just don't know where others have been, what they have been through to cause them to act in a certain way that you may not understand.

As you walk the path of your goals and dreams, you will encounter thousands of people; most encounters will be brief and of no consequence, but there will be encounters where you have a chance to learn a lesson. Always look for the "nugget!"

Regardless of a person's intelligence, they have something to teach you. Everyone has something magical that excites them, which is their passion. You should strive to see from another's point of view in a non-judgmental way. This will benefit you and the other person.

By being understanding and attentive to the person you are talking with, you are able to maximize each interaction. You never know when someone will share knowledge that will change your life. You also never know when you will give someone else knowledge that will change their life. Imagine what it would be like to change someone's life for the better!

By trying to see another's viewpoint, you can maximize your benefit, maximize the benefit to others, and minimize damage created by conflicts.

When there seems to be conflict, it becomes even more important for you to step into the other person's shoes to see a situation from their position. Preventing and resolving conflicts can be a rewarding way to learn life lessons. The only way this will happen is when you are respectful and do your best to understand.

Principle 32: Be Able to See Things From Other's Viewpoints. You can gain more from your interactions with others by taking an open approach and not judging someone because of how they look and how you perceive their intelligence, their experience, age, or income level.

Notes

BE WILLING TO ADMIT WHEN YOU ARE WRONG

Chapter 33 Be Willing to Admit When You Are Wrong

Be willing to admit you are wrong. One of the worst things people can do is to live in a right versus wrong world. Often, there is more than one correct answer to a problem, but if you have made an honest mistake, admit it and take steps to correct the situation so you can keep moving forward.

ONE OF THE MOST NEGATIVE BEHAVIORS YOU CAN DEVELOP IS TO ALWAYS BLAME OTHERS FOR YOU OWN FAILINGS. Successful people can fail their way to success because they take chances, experience failure and learn from it. So, why pretend that you don't make mistakes?

Another way to think about being wrong is that you made a mistake. Perhaps, you didn't have as much information about a situation as you needed to be fully informed. Maybe you were in a hurry to move ahead and didn't do the work in the current step to properly complete it.

If you know you are wrong and admit it, you have taken the first step to resolving the issue and moving on. To hold on to your mistaken opinion or misrepresented fact only makes your situation worse and draws it out longer. It stalls your progress.

If you know you made a mistake, why would you continue to want to do something wrong?

It is natural human tendency to want to be smart, to be right, and to feel important. When you are wrong or make mistakes, you feel like you are not smart, that you are not important. This is especially true in front of other people. It is just not true!

A common misconception you may have about being wrong or making mistakes is that you feel like your intelligence is directly tied to being right and not making mistakes. This is a primitive way of thinking because unless something is going to cause harm, it doesn't matter. Most mistakes can be figured out or fixed when you notice them.

Imagine being coached on how to play the guitar or learning the sport of golf. When you first start learning, there is no way you will not make mistakes. The coach knows when you make a mistake, even if you don't realize that you have. That is true when you are learning about being successful and running a business as well. More experienced people who know about your path to your goals and dreams may think a step you take is a mistake. If you realize you are wrong, but won't admit it, eventually it will be shown to be true and what little bit of pride you thought you were keeping will be lost anyway.

I had an employee who got a piece of equipment stuck while doing his job. For over two hours, he worked alone to fix his mistake, with no luck. Finally, he called to admit his mistake and ask for help. Within five minutes, with four people, we freed the piece of equipment. In my mind, wasting two hours of time was much worse than just admitting a mistake!

To be wrong and to make mistakes are expected. You have to fall off of your bike many times before you learn how to ride it. You have to fall off your skateboard, strike out in baseball, and miss the goal in soccer.

With so much information in the world, it is impossible to know it all, so if you are wrong, who cares? Admit it.

Principle 33: Be Willing to Admit It When You Are Wrong. Mistakes happen, and that is OK. Be willing to admit if you made a mistake. Most people will have a hard time admitting it, but you will set yourself apart, in a good way, when you readily admit you took a wrong direction. Just as someone can be respected for being right, to admit a wrong can also gain respect.

EVEN IF YOU SAY THE WRONG THING, YOU WILL STILL GET RECIPROCAL ATTENTION, YOU WON'T APPEAR ARROGANT OR NOT CARING. THIS IS THE ROOT OF MUTUAL RESPECT, UNDERSTANDING AND COOPERATION.

HAVE A GENUINE INTEREST IN OTHER PEOPLE.

Chapter 34. Have a Genuine Interest In Other People

In a world where something is always demanding our attention, many people don't really listen to what other people are saying. In many ways, it can work against you if you are not hearing what someone else is saying. Not paying attention to what someone says because you are thinking more about what you are going to say next can set you up for conflict and misunderstanding you should try to avoid.

This principle goes right to the fact that people want to feel that they are important. They believe that what they have to say is important and can give you value.

Having a genuine interest in other people's interests, opinions, and ideas shows respect for the person speaking. How can you expect others to show interest and respect toward you if you don't show it to them?

Worthwhile accomplishments will require the help of others. Whether they spend five minutes giving you advice or work full time for you, having a genuine interest in others is the first step toward showing that you respect them.

By ignoring the opinion and interests of others, not only do you come off as arrogant, but you also make them think that you don't care about them.

As I have been teaching throughout this book, one interaction with someone can change their life. Ask yourself if you are building up or tearing down through your interactions. By showing genuine interest in their ideas and opinions, you give people the opportunity to respect yours. There will always be people who are jerks and aren't interested in what you have to say or teach. The important thing is you won't know unless you do your part to show respect to them.

Make sure you genuinely listen to people. If your mind is not focusing on what someone is saying to you, you can easily misunderstand what they are telling you. A parent could be telling you something important, but you are too busy watching TV, or playing a game to really hear them. They even could ask, "Did you hear me?" All you really heard was, "BLAH, BLAH, BLAH, BLAH". You have now set yourself up for potential failure. You could miss something cool, you could really get yelled at, or you could be late for something you really want to do.

In the real world, missed opportunities can be HUGE. By practicing this principle, you open more doors, whereas not practicing this will close doors.

Principle 34: Have a Genuine Interest in Other People. Listening and showing interest in what others are saying or are interested in is the root of mutual respect, understanding, and cooperation.

Notes

GOAL!
GOAL!
GOAL!
MAYBE IT'S NOT A GOOD GOAL.
NEVER GIVE UP

Chapter 35 Never Give Up

Never giving up is how you reach your goals and dreams. Nothing in this world is perfect or easy. Know that you will go through some tough times if you try to accomplish anything worthwhile. But like a rainy day, the sun will shine again, and you will be back on the right path to achieving your goals and dreams.

The key to never giving up is to focus on the big picture, your end goals and dreams; to focus on the things that matter—that can make all the difference in your success.

There will be times when you are on fire to work towards your goals. Every step you take seems to work in your favor. You have lots of energy and enthusiasm. But, there will be times when it seems as if everything you attempt doesn't work. You will feel tired and doubtful that you are even doing the right thing. You may experience negative feelings that you just can't do this; you just can't succeed. These times are what adults call life's ups and downs.

This principle is written as an intervention to negative thoughts and is one you should return to and refamiliarize yourself with throughout your journey. It's your pep talk to remind you that you are doing the right things by following all of the principles of this book.

The Power of Affirmations taught you that the mind only knows what you tell it. When was the last time that you visited your written goals and read them out loud? If you are feeling like you are in one of life's downs, start practicing affirmations again if you stopped. See the words you wrote or write new ones to adjust your goal. Hear your voice reading your goals, feel the vibration of the words in your throat, and feel them in your heart. Believe that this is your life's grandest plan at this moment.

Remember that consistency will get you through periods of ups and downs. By making it a point to take steps each day toward your goals and dreams, you are always moving in the right direction. Even if you are not motivated, feel distracted, are uninspired, and just plain tired, showing up and putting in your time is how you will reach your mark.

Sometimes, life is tough. You find yourself in a tough situation where you take three steps forward, then get knocked two steps back. You take another three steps forward, then get knocked back five steps. Then, you take one step and get knocked back more steps. It seems like you just can't get ahead on the path to your dreams.

The key is to keep getting back up and not giving up. Even if you take one small step forward, you are moving in the right direction. Experience will make you strong in the knowledge that you won't get knocked back as much, that you can recover from missteps and make major strides.

If you allow yourself to get side tracked, or you put your goals and dreams down for a while, it's OK. You can always pick them back up.

What do professional athletes do when they don't feel well or are tired? They still must get up to train and workout and push themselves through it. A day off from training to them means stepping backwards. Their career is built on being able to perform as an athlete.

As you learned with the principle Be Willing to Admit When You Are Wrong, sometimes you have to assess the situation and change the direction of your path if the direction you are going isn't going to work, or you were going down the wrong path. It's ok because you know to focus on your big goals and dreams and realize that how you achieve them may change, and that you can be flexible with how everything will unfold. You have to focus on the big picture of accomplishing something worthwhile with your life.

Principle 35: Never Give Up. It may take years to accomplish your dreams and goals, but don't give up! Know in your heart what you want and keep making steps toward making it happen every day.

8-10 HRS OF SLEEP NIGHTLY IS THE RECOMMENDED TIME FOR OPTIMAL RESULTS IN HEALTH, FOCUS, GRADES, CREATIVITY AND PERFORMANCE

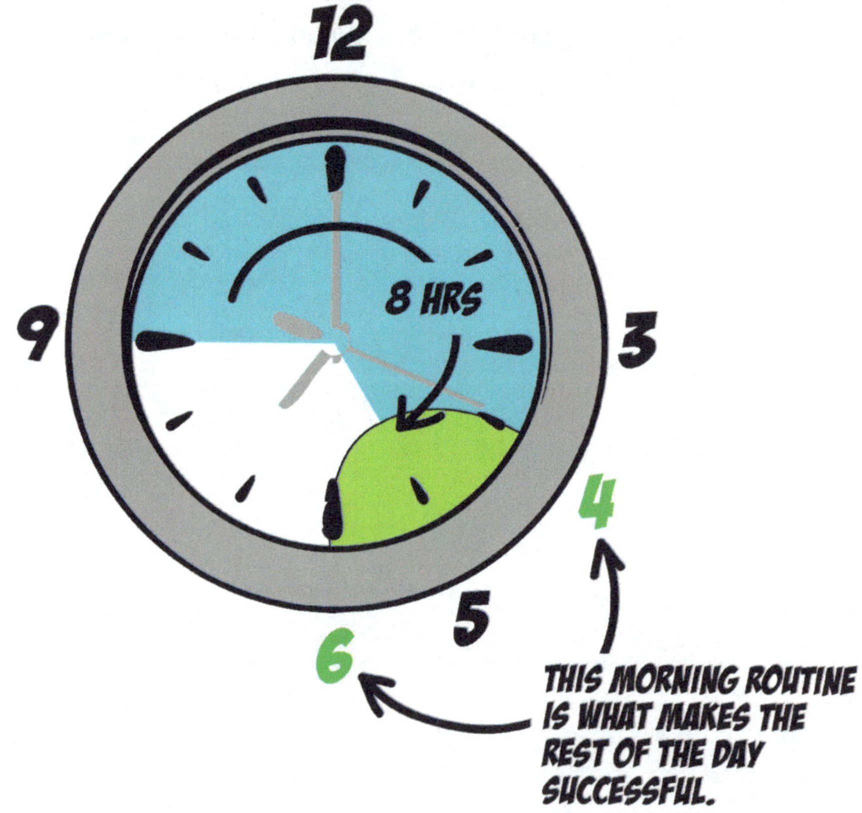

YOUR MORNING ROUTINE CAN BE POWERFUL.

Chapter 36 Your Morning Routine Can Be Powerful

Just like food and water, the body needs enough sleep to function at its best. By going to bed early, and getting a good night's sleep, you allow your body time to recover and recharge. The secret is to get up and follow a set routine that sets your day up for success.

Early morning is often a good time to find several uninterrupted hours of time you can put toward following these principles to accomplish your goals and dreams. As you mature and take on more responsibility, time to do things other than your obligations becomes scarce. By rising early, you gain back some of that precious time.

People are different when it comes to getting enough sleep, and the amount of sleep your body will need will vary over your lifetime. On average, eight hours of sleep is considered a good amount of sleep to get. This means that if you want to get up at 5:00 to work on your goals, make sure to be in bed by 9:00 to get those eight hours of sleep.

Many of the world's most successful people will claim that being an early riser has helped them to succeed. By rising early, you can write in your journal, read up on your area of expertise, or return emails. Others will meditate, read affirmations, exercise, workout, or walk their dog. It is up to you to know how to use that time. It is also up to you to be consistent.

Studies on better sleep habits have shown you can improve your health, grades, memory, creativity, and a better attention span. Even taking naps is helpful! Some companies have spaces for employees to go during the workday to take a quick nap. They realize that some people will function better by getting sleep when it's needed, even if it's during working hours.

A perfect morning routine may look like this:

Up early starting with some meditation (Visualization)

Reading your affirmation statements

Exercising

Reading a book

Planning your day

Accomplishing the most important thing first

Principle 36: Your Morning Routine Can Be Powerful. Get a good night's rest and wake up early. People who sleep well are more likely to have the energy to go after their goals and dreams. Also, make sure to create a powerful routine that you consistently follow—ideally one that follows some type of meditation, affirmation review, reading, and exercise. It is up to you to find what works best for you.

Notes

THEY BOTH HAVE MORE THAN THEY WOULD HAVE WITHOUT GIVING.

NO GIVING

GIVING HAS TAKEN PLACE

THERE IS POWER IN GIVING.

Chapter 37 There is Power in Giving

Many successful people claim that giving is one of the most important things you can do on your journey to accomplishing your goals and dreams.

People who have had tremendous financial success give away their time and their money!

People who do this are called philanthropists. The word philanthropy comes from 2 Greek words, phil (Loving) and Anthropos (Mankind)—a love of mankind. But, you don't have to wait until you are wildly successful to become a philanthropist; you can have a love of mankind whatever your financial status and give away your time and money.

Why do you think they do it?

It goes back to The Golden Rule, where what you put out into the universe returns to you, like a boomerang. Giving to others makes you feel good because you know that those who receive your gifts feel good. You want to show your appreciation for those who helped your success by helping others.

Some people will donate their time, some people will donate money, some do both!

By naturally being a giver, you will notice people seem to be giving and helping you. Usually, it will come in a most unexpected way, but it will come. You shouldn't be giving just because you want help yourself.

Unfortunately, the world is imperfect. There are many givers in the world, but there are also takers.

As a giver, you must be on the lookout for the takers. You will give, and they will expect more. They will strive to get as much from you as possible, then move on to the next person to take from them without a second thought of repaying the gift or passing it on to someone else.

It is OK to give to a taker. You must realize it is not their fault that you are a giver and they are a taker. You just don't want to make the mistake of continuing to give to a taker, as it will drain your energy, and create negative energy within you. It will also allow the taker to continue their greedy habit.

Principle 37: There is Power in Giving. Successful people have learned there is power in being a giver of your time and money to help others; however, you must realize that there are also takers who never consider giving back in appreciation for their success.

Notes

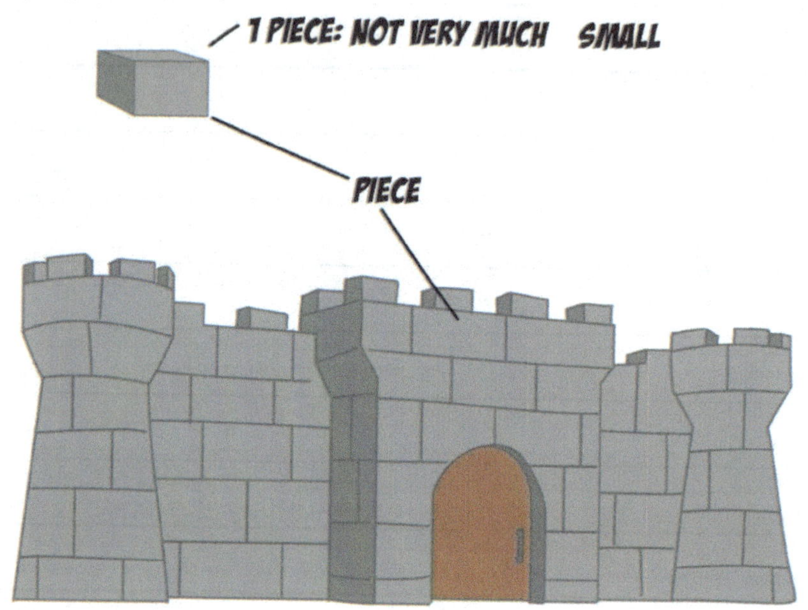

PIECE FORTRESS: VERY BIG + COMPLEX. MADE FROM INDIVIDUAL PIECES

SMALL THINGS MATTER BIG

Chapter 38. Small Things Matter Big

When going after your life goals and dreams, it is important to see the big picture. You also have to realize that the little things add up to the big things.

Think about Legos. One little piece is small and doesn't mean much, but when arranged with lots of other Legos, you can create some amazing stuff. I've seen people create entire cities, spaceships, and towers. Have you ever heard of Lego Land? It is an entire theme park made from millions and millions of Legos. One Lego, as small as it is, is still part of the whole.

That is an example of how small objects can be combined to make big ones. The same is true of small actions. Many small, positive actions can add up to a big positive outcome. The opposite is also true: Many small negative actions can have big negative results.

When writing this book, I made major progress by working every morning at 5:30 a.m. I would work in waves, where sometimes I had major progress, other times I made virtually no progress. With other demands of life happening around me, I would sometimes review a chapter at lunch, or take the time to explain my concept to a friend. Five or ten minutes of review or explaining seems insignificant when considering the vast amount of information in The Prodigy Kid system. The point is, even when it seemed like there weren't enough hours in a day to do one more thing, I would still make small and consistent steps writing my book. I had the bigger picture of producing this book in my mind. If I had not taken those small steps, you wouldn't be reading this!

Keep the bigger picture in your mind. Even when you don't think you have time, make it a point every day to take small steps toward your goals and dreams. Research some stuff, throw some balls, watch some videos, write some stuff in your Magic Notebook, talk to someone about what you are doing, and find people who have done what you are trying to do. As long as you act every day, you are working towards your big picture.

Principle 38: Small Things Matter Big. By taking care of the small things each day, the big things take care of themselves.

Notes

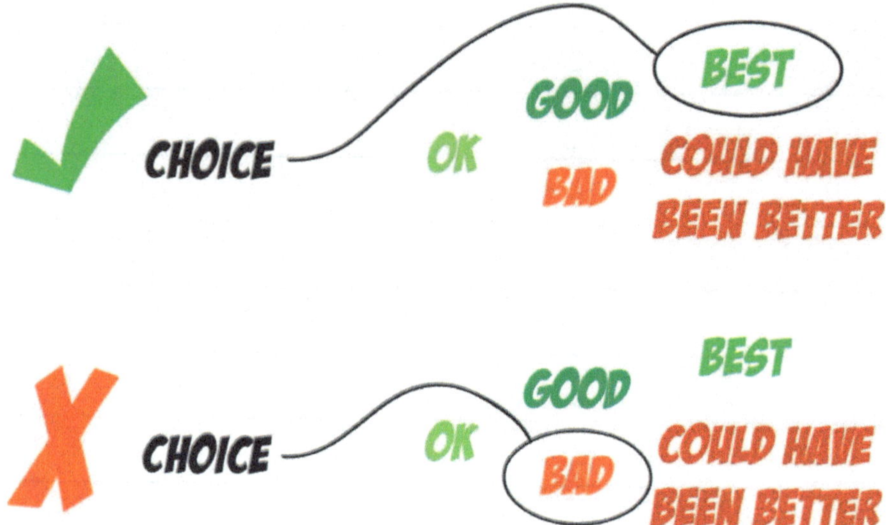

TAKE THE TIME TO MAKE GOOD CHOICES!

Chapter 39 Take the Time To Make Good Choices

How your life turns out depends on the choices that you make. We are given the gift of having the ability to choose. Some things, unfortunately, are beyond our control. It is our duty to make the best of those things that we can control by making good choices.

You have to ask yourself these three questions: "Is this the right thing? Will this help or hurt me? Is this something that will lead to good consequences?"

By focusing on each choice that you make, you become more aware of the consequences for each choice. Of course, not all choices have a great impact. For example, if you choose to put your left shoe on before your right one, it won't really matter; but not doing your homework is a choice that has big consequences in the future. In the short term, you may get free time to do what you want with the consequence of a bad homework grade; but as time goes on, consistently not doing homework means long term negative consequences.

Over time, your grades become worse. You don't develop the habit of doing homework, so in time, your grades spiral down from good, to poor, to really bad. Good grades aren't the only reason to do homework. Gaining the knowledge learned from the homework lessons and developing the discipline of doing those things you don't want to do for some future gain are all part of the big picture to achieving your goals. It is a discipline that transfers to many areas of your life.

Once you enter the workforce and are completely responsible for all aspects of paying for your life, and everything in it, your opportunity to make good choices becomes infinite.

When you decide that you want to go after your goals and dreams, it will require you making lots of good choices. In a world where you can easily be distracted in a million different directions, focusing on making each choice a good one will help to keep you disciplined.

That is why you learned the principle to write down your goals and dreams and review them daily. It is a discipline that reinforces what is important to you, and as important decisions come up, you will make choices that keep you on the journey to your goals.

With the gift of choice comes much responsibility. Everyone in life is where they are based on decisions they have made. You must own your choices and be accountable. While sometimes things that are not within your control happen, those things that are will be up to you to make the best choice.

Principle 39: Take the Time to Make Good Choices. By asking yourself questions like, "Will this hurt or benefit me? Is this the best option? What will give me the greatest result?", you are more likely to make good choices that lead you to your goals. By knowing what you want in your life and making the right decision one step at a time, you can eventually arrive at your ultimate destination.

Notes

NO GRATITUDE

MONEY, FAME AWESOME LIFE, TRAVEL, ETC.

=

UNHAPPY

GRATEFUL

MONEY, FAME AWESOME LIFE, TRAVEL, ETC.

=

HAPPY

GRATEFUL

NOT A LOT OF MONEY, NO FAME, AVERAGE LIFE, NO TRAVEL, ETC.

=

HAPPY

YOU HAVE TO HAVE "GRATITUDE" FOR OPPORTUNITIES

Chapter 40. You Have to Have Gratitude for Opportunities!

Self-esteem and self-confidence are key to success in life. To be happy with yourself and your life should be everyone's goal, part of that is being grateful (happy) for all you have.

Happiness is strongly associated with good self-esteem and self-confidence. When you feel self-confident and good about yourself, you are also likely to be happy with how you look, your own intelligence, relationships with your friends and family, how much money you have—everything.

In, "The Prodigy Kid", we have talked about what we can and can't control in different situations. Lack of control is associated with being unhappy and frustrated. What The Prodigy Kid teaches is that when you beat yourself up over things you cannot control, you divert your energy from the positive direction towards your goals. The key is to change the things that you can work on and accept what you cannot control. To achieve this discipline is a big step towards happiness in your life.

Success without happiness and gratitude is not really success.

Money, fame, talent, and good looks are all temporary forms of success, which mean nothing if happiness is not a part of your life. When you are drawn to what you love, your passion contributes to your sense of happiness and wellbeing.

If you live honestly, and try do the right thing, you will be true to yourself! If you are dishonest and do the wrong thing, deep in your heart, you will know the truth. Real happiness will come from staying on the right track even when nobody is watching.

Achieving a life with happiness may not always not make sense. Here are some examples why that is true.

Let's say that skipping homework or not cleaning your room makes you happy. Should you embrace those moments of happiness? As logical as that may sound, it doesn't work and if you have made it this far in The Prodigy Kid, you already know that. You have learned that in the long term, not doing homework leads to future unhappiness with poor grades, and fewer opportunities. In the long term, having a dirty room leads to future unhappiness with a disorganized life.

By falling for instant gratification, your future happiness is affected. Instant gratification is the desire for immediate fulfillment of a need, desire or urge. It's when you do what makes you happy now, knowing it possibly could harm you or make you unhappy in the future.

Practicing delayed gratification means you may have to wait to get what you want and waiting makes you feel anxious or nervous. As you gain experience in delaying gratification, some of those feelings go away because you know there is the promise of a more permanent happiness in the future.

There are some situations where instant gratification makes sense. If you are hungry and feel like you can't do your best unless you eat, maybe you should eat. Too much delayed gratification can lead to instant unhappiness! Imagine that. Life experience will teach you that there must be a balance between focusing on your goals and enjoying life, so that you don't regret a life of sacrifice when you ultimately do achieve your goals.

Principle 40: You Have to Have Gratitude for Opportunities
Seek a balance of happiness and gratitude now, as well as in the future. Don't always delay gratification; reward yourself along the way to achieving your ultimate goals and dreams and always be happy for what you have, even if it's not very much.

Appendix: Prodigy Kid Daily Success Affirmation:

- I know that I can achieve my goals and dreams in life, and I now promise to take the action needed to make them happen!
- I have written down a clear statement of what my main goals and dreams are in life, as if they've already come true.
- I know that by creating a movie in my mind of my dreams and goals, as if they have already happened, and focusing on them for a few minutes daily, that I will be drawn to trusting that I can make them real.
- I know that if I read my goals out loud and revise them daily, that I will be creating a clear picture in my mind of the person I intend to become.
- I understand that thinking BIG makes it easier to be successful than having mediocre goals and dreams.
- I understand that interacting well with people is KEY to my success. I hereby promise to learn all that I can about people skills and the art of working successfully with other people. I will master those skills by practicing them until they become second nature to me.
- I promise to be honest and always consider the viewpoints of other people.
- I will become an excellent reader and strive for a true love for learning.

- I will not be afraid to make mistakes. I will learn from them and will try not to make them again.
- I understand that attitude is 85% of success and promise to have a positive view of the world without anger or stress.
- I will get plenty of sleep.
- I will eat healthy and drink lots of water because I will need a strong healthy body to accomplish my goals and dreams.
- I will be on time for meetings and make myself presentable because these are simple things that make success easier, regardless of skills or special abilities.
- I will always be thankful for my life and all that is in it, regardless of how bad a situation may be, knowing that there are those who have it worse than I do. I will show my gratitude by giving back to others when I am able.
- I will sign my name to these affirmations, read them out loud each day, and memorize them, knowing that they will help change my thoughts and actions, to help me become the person I need to be to accomplish my dreams and goals.

Acknowledgements:

There have been many people that have given me their time to listen to my ideas that I've had about this book and, "The Prodigy Kid Blueprint", you were one of the many who gave even one minute of time, I THANK YOU! There are too many for me to remember and list, so if your name is not listed, I apologize in advance!

Thank you to Nate. Without you, "The Prodigy Kid", would never have made it to the world. Regardless of where you end up in life, and what you choose to do with yourself, you will ALWAYS be my Prodigy Kid!

I've got to thank my mom for being a dreamer and always leaving books around for me to find when I was younger like, "Awaken the Giant Within", "Think and Grow Rich", "The Power of Positive Thinking", and always showing up to my house later in life with books that you think will interest me!

Thank you to my dad for being hard working and success driven. You have provided me a great example of how to be legit and make it happen!

Tim Emeis, what can I say? I have always considered you my, "Rich Dad/ neighbor!" Thanks for all you did in the early days!

Thank you to Bethann Vetter, thanks for helping me copyright this book. Your coaching saved my life, and I will be forever grateful and indebted to you.

Renee, thank you for listening to my ideas and being the first one to read the rough draft of the book! Your input was awesome!

Celeste, thank you for talking with me. It was you that put the fire under this project by validating that I was on to something BIG!

Thanks for Jesse Walker and Daniel Iriarte for stepping up big in the traditional business while I was sick and working on this.

Thank you to all of Nate's teachers for giving your working lives to help kids learn! Mrs. Marina, Mr. Gilbert, Mrs. Copeland, Mrs. Swetman, Mrs. Nall, Miss Cusak, Mrs. Kyne, and Mrs. Arnett.

Thank you to Nate's Principal, Mrs. Kimball, for your KIND WORDS and support. It meant A LOT to me when I was going through one of the worst times of my life with my health and finances.

A BIG shoutout to Parker Woodward for getting me back on track! Thanks to Josh Forti and his "Master Story Workshop". Thank you Luis Camejo for helping me setup TheProdigyKidPodcast!

Thanks to my teacher friends for reviewing and grading the book. Ali, Alex, Sara, Sydney, Tina, and AJ.

Like I said, so many people have listened, given ideas, offered to buy books! That book buying offer helps too! It made me keep pushing! The following are some of the many others that deserve thanks. PLEASE FORGIVE ME IF I FORGOT TO ADD YOU; LET ME KNOW, AND I WILL ADD YOU TO THE NEXT VERSION!

Thanks to: Travis Dixon, Dr. Flint McGlaughlin, Laura, Stella, Meadow, Caroline, Heather, Alina, Erin, Kenya, Alyssa, Jon, Russell Brunson, Dan Kennedy, Justin H, Billy K, Dr. Colleen Sabol-Olitsky, Corrine H, Jason D, The Jon Gharners, The Mauras, Jan B, The Peacos, Jesse H, John F, Brig H, Lana C, Paul D, Gesina!, Pokey!, Analin M, Nathan B, Laura , Karen B, Dylan A, Lauren W, Parker W, Ben E, The UNF Center for Entrepreneurship and Innovation, and dozens more—I just can't remember all of you at this moment! As I was writing this, Joe M and Barbara K, and Barbara W jumped in there too!

This is where I have to add a disclaimer! I've gotten the principles in this book from reading books, studying successful people, asking questions, and applying them to my life. This book is presented solely for educational and entertainment purposes. Use your best judgement on how to apply these principles in your life to your benefit. Of course, we offer no guarantee that by reading this book, you will be successful. We do, however, guarantee that you will be presented 40 very powerful ways of thinking that you can choose to apply to your life to potentially become very successful.

We cannot be held liable or responsible to any person or entity with respect to any loss or incidental or consequential damages caused, or alleged to have been caused, directly or indirectly, by the information or principles contained herein. For example, the principle of honesty (Chapter 14) says to be honest. If you did something wrong and then were honest about it and it ruined your life, it's not our fault! Just saying!

And remember, BE A PRODIGY KID, CHANGE YOUR WORLD!

Prodigy Kid, LLC

3948 South 3rd Street #375

Jacksonville Beach, Fl 32250

ProdigyKidBlueprint.com

TheProdigyKidPodcast.com

A note to parents:

Congratulations on getting The Prodigy Kid book for your future Prodigy Kid!

Learning the concepts found in this book at a young age can set your child up for extraordinary success if they learn how to put them into ACTION over their lifetime.

The Prodigy Kid book is the "mindset" part of The Prodigy Kid Blueprint!

Go to ProdigyKidBlueprint.com for the next ACTION steps to start YOUR Prodigy Kid on the journey of creating an EXTRORDINARY LIFE!

Made in the USA
Columbia, SC
16 October 2023

24136423R00098